CURRENT AFRICAN ISSUES No 67

RAINBOWS, PYTHONS AND WATERFALLS

Heritage, poverty and sacrifice among the Busoga, Uganda

Author
Terje Oestigaard

NORDISKA AFRIKAINSITUTET
The Nordic Africa Institute

UPPSALA 2019

INDEXING TERMS:

Cultural heritage
Religion
Traditional culture
Water
Rivers
Rain
Mythology
Rituals
Belief
Nile River
Uganda

Rainbows, pythons and waterfalls :
Heritage, poverty and sacrifice among the Busoga, Uganda
Current African Issues No 67

Author Terje Oestigaard

ISSN 0280-2171
ISBN 978-91-7106-847-7 print-on-demand version
ISBN 978-91-7106-848-4 pdf e-book

© 2019 The author and the Nordic Africa Institute

Production editor: Henrik Alfredsson, the Nordic Africa Institute
Layout: Marianne Engblom, Ateljé Idé.

Front cover: © Terje Oestigaard
Back cover: © Terje Oestigaard

THE NORDIC AFRICA INSTITUTE (Nordiska Afrikainstitutet) is a centre for research, knowledge, policy advice and information on Africa. Based in Uppsala, Sweden, we are a government agency, funded jointly by Sweden, Finland and Iceland.

The opinions expressed in this volume are those of the author and do not necessarily reflect the views of the Nordic Africa Institute.

Print editions are available for purchase, more information can be found at the NAI web page www.nai.uu.se.

Contents

Acknowledgements

This book is mainly about Mesoké and a rainmaking ritual conducted in 2017, when a goat was sacrificed; the ritual was intended to secure and procure the life-giving rains at a crucial time when a devastating drought was predicted.

There is one person in particular I would like to thank, and that is Mary Itanda. I am immensely grateful to have met her and to have had the chance to talk to her when I have been in Uganda. Mary is the healer embodying or incarnating the main spirits and gods residing in the Itanda Falls on the White Nile, near the outlet of Lake Victoria at Jinja. She is not only the medium for the mighty Itanda god, but the rain-god Mesoké also uses her as his ritual specialist. I also extend my thanks to the other healers who answered my questions, and in particular Jaja Bujagali and Jaja Kiyira.

In Jinja, I would like to thank Moses Mugweri and Oki Simon for practical help and assistance. I am also grateful to Richard K. Gonza and the Cultural Research Centre. Throughout the years I have benefited greatly from discussions with Richard, and the centre's studies of the cultural heritage of Busoga have been an invaluable source of information. For more in-depth information not only on the Busoga cosmology, but also on the Nile from its sources to the sea over a 5,000-year span, I refer to my book *The Religious Nile: Water, Ritual and Society since Ancient Egypt* (I.B. Tauris, London, 2018).

I would thank the Nordic Africa Institute in Uppsala, Sweden, and all my colleagues there; in particular Henrik Alfredsson deserves special thanks not only for making the maps used in this and other publications, but also for doing an impressive job with the layout. Also, Marianne Engblom has done a great job with the layout. I would like to thank prof. Terje Tvedt for inspiring discussion throughout the years, Dr. Tore Sætersdal and the WaSo-programme for support, Patience Mususa for discussions about the role of culture studies in African developments; and the Forum for Africa Studies at Uppsala University, where I presented and discussed parts of these approaches. Lastly, I should thank Clive Liddiard for commenting on the language.

Needless to say, I am solely responsible for any errors or misinterpretations of empirical data – and of course, for the interpretations and arguments put forward in this book.

Terje Oestigaard
Uppsala, 10 June 2019

It is at times of hardship that the gods may help – and are expected to help – if the right rituals are conducted by the right people in the right way. And as it turned out, the gods did not ignore their children and devotees: the good rains came after a rainmaking ritual and a sacrifice.

Chapter 1

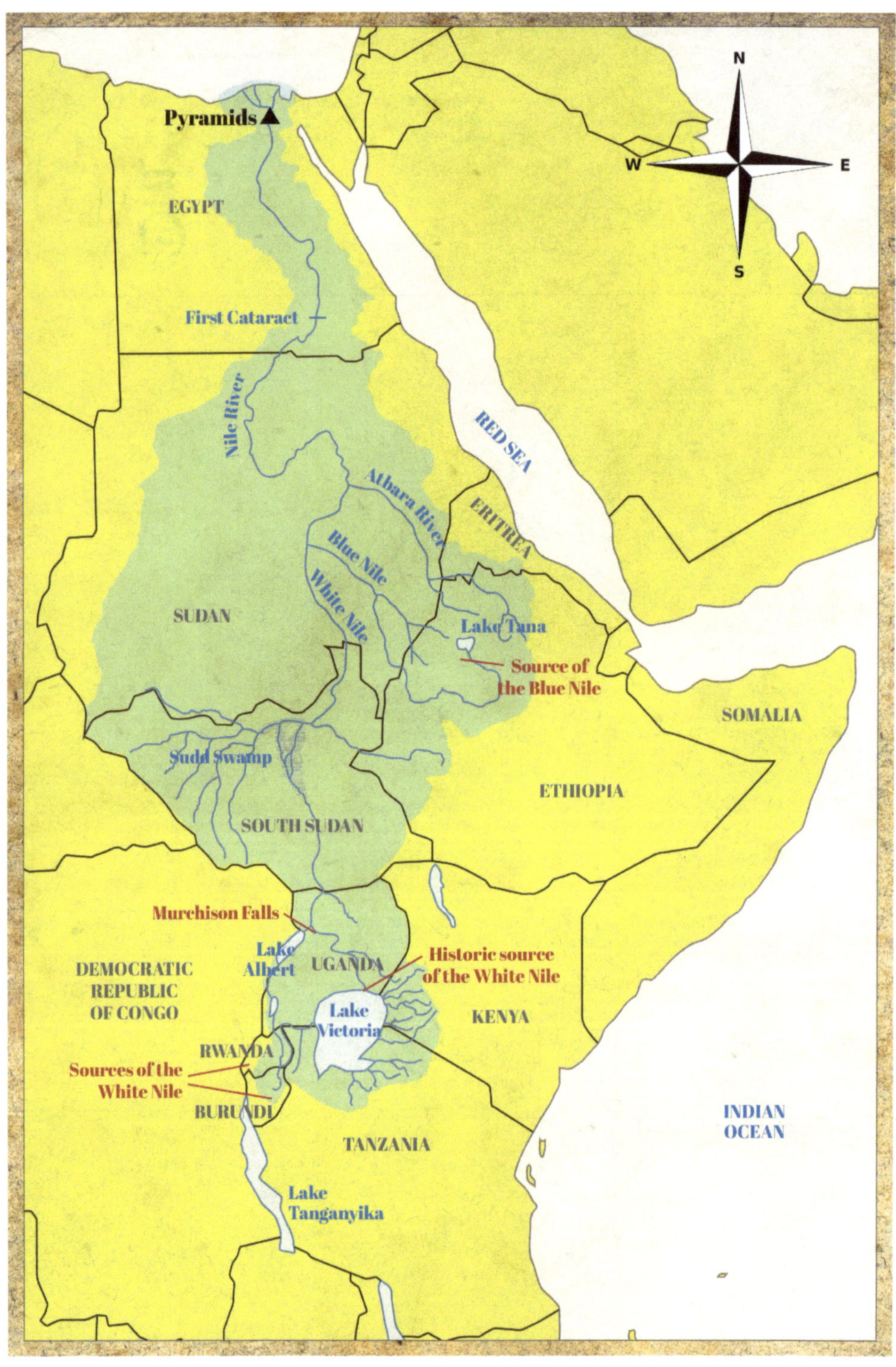

Figure 1a Map of the Nile Basin and the historic source of the White Nile and Lake Victoria in Uganda. Map: Henrik Alfredsson, Nordic Africa Institute.

1. Mythology of hydrology

'… across the millennia the rainbow has been venerated as god and goddess, feared as demon and pestilence, trusted as battle omen, and used as an optical proving ground. The rainbow image is woven into the fabric of both our past and present, but its very familiarity today renders it nearly invisible. For all of us, a fresh look at the rainbow seems well worth-while, especially given that the bow spans some modern divides between arts and science.[1]'

A famine framing the importance of the gods

On 20 February 2017, and for the first time anywhere in the world over the past six years, the United Nations declared a famine in parts of South Sudan. Although the famine was largely a result of war and political mismanagement, it was also caused by a drought in this part of the Nile Basin. Uganda, the neighbouring country to South Sudan, is usually lush and verdant with plentiful rain; but even there the rains had been erratic and inadequate over the previous 4–5 months, and the harvests had started to fail. Drought was creeping southwards from South Sudan and the prospects looked grim. The rains would most likely fail, leading to subsequent harvest failure and human misery and suffering.

The rainbow, the python and making rain

Approximately 30 kilometres north of the historic source of the White Nile in Uganda, or the outlet of Lake Victoria and the former Owen Falls, are the Itanda Falls (Figure 1). The waterfalls in this area used to be like a string of pearls: first Ripon Falls and Owen Falls, then Bujagali Falls some 8 kilometres from the source, and then Itanda or Kalagala Falls. The Victoria Nile (or the Nile flowing from Lake Victoria) separates the Buganda Kingdom to the west and the much smaller Busoga Kingdom to the east. Although the same water-falls, they are called Kalagala on the Buganda side and Itanda on the Busoga side of the river.

In each of the falls live innumerable water gods, river spirits and ancestors, and the main gods incarnate or embody themselves in one respective healer: Jaja Kiyira (at the source), Jaja Bujagali and Mary Itanda. While many of these gods and spirits (and the damming processes) have been discussed elsewhere,[2] the spirits at Itanda Falls, which are not dammed, are of utmost cosmological importance. Not only do some of the most powerful river-gods in the Busoga Kingdom live in these waterfalls, but so does the rain-god Mesoké. In times of hardship, with a possible drought coming among the Busoga and a famine in the neighbouring country, a rain-god is more important than a river-god. From one perspective – and in particular at this time, with an emerging crisis – Mesoké was the most important god in the kingdom, which desperately needed the right rains to fall in the right amount in the right places. Mesoké also embodies Mary Itanda and uses her as his medium.

I first met Mary Itanda in 2013, and over the next five years I visited her whenever I was in Uganda, conducting fieldwork along the Nile in the Busoga Kingdom. It has always been a pleasure to meet Mary and talk with her, and I hope (and believe) she feels the same way; but when I was back on 3 March 2017, it was different. Mary was upset at the new, completed Isimba Dam downstream of the Itanda waterfalls: the reservoir's tail end would potentially flood parts of the surrounding area and could even impact the Itanda (Kalagala) waterfalls themselves.

With a possible drought coming, it felt like something of a luxury to have the opportunity to ask about river spirits and rain-gods. I was wrong: river spirits and rain-gods are real life, and it is at precisely times like this that one needs the gods more than ever. If they cannot help when people desperately need the life-giving rains, when are they needed? It is at times of hardship that the gods may help – and are expected to help – if the right rituals are conducted by the right people in the right way. And as it turned out, the gods did not ignore their children and devotees: the good rains came after a rainmaking ritual and a sacrifice. Rituals and religions matter. And from an academic point of view, so do cultural and natural heritage, tangible and intangible heritage.

This book is about some of the answers Mary provided, the rituals she conducted and the questions they raised. From a non-religious perspective, it seems impossible for a local healer or rainmaker to procure the necessary rains through prayer, sacrifice and ritual. Still, if one focuses only on the functional outcome of the rituals – rain (and nothing is more important than rain when there is drought) – one misses the importance of the broader role and the social function of tradition in culture and society, and of cultural and natural heritage.

As a healer or medium, Mary may be incarnated by several of the gods residing in the Itanda waterfalls – but not at the same time (Figure 2). If the divinities want to convey a message to the community and the believers, they may possess Mary and instruct her and the devotees. Likewise, if the devotees want to communicate any wishes or concerns to the deities, they may go through Mary, who (in a possessed state) conveys the messages to the gods.

The river-god Itanda is the mightiest god living in the Itanda Falls; but another very strong god is the angry and hot-tempered rain-god Mesoké. Although Mary is not a traditional rainmaker as such (since she primarily embodies the Itanda god), she may also intervene in these matters and be part of the domains of rain. Having visited Mary before and asked about the divine pantheon, I had new questions for her. One in particular was this: why is there a rain-god living in the river and the waterfalls? Why does the rain-god not live in the sky or heaven? Intuitively, there seemed a contradiction in the representation of two different water phenomena. Of course, I was wrong. Mary Itanda not only revealed the underlying logic (which was indeed very logical), but showed it to be a beautiful cosmology, shining like the rainbow itself and linking the rain-god, the good rains, the pythons and the waterfalls.

Figure 2. Mary Itanda in her ritual hut next to the Itanda waterfalls. Photo: Terje Oestigaard.

Cosmologically and hydrologically, the water-world shared the same logic. The python has a shape and colours like the rainbow, and together they connect and complete the hydrological cycle. While the main task (both divine and profane) of a rain-god is to provide the necessary and life-giving rains to his devotees, even a rain-god needs to make rain. There is no rain just there in the sky: a rain-god needs to procure it – bring it – before he can give it to the needy devotees, or to those who deserve it, by dint of having been obedient and made the auspicious sacrifices.

Usually when we see a rainbow, it is after rain on sunny days; but this represents only half of the cosmological and hydrological cycle. Before the rains can be released from the sky as a divine gift, making a beautiful rainbow in the sky, Mesoké himself has to bring the waters to the sky. And that happens through the rainbow. Each morning on clear days, a rainbow rises from the waterfalls when the sun rises. From the Itanda waterfalls rises a perfect, beautiful rainbow. The cascading torrents of water in the waterfalls splash the water high into the air. Literally, one can see the water droplets being dragged up to heaven. The rainbow is like a reversed waterfall, filling heaven with water. This is the work of Mesoké, and through the rainbow he sucks water up into the sky. The same procedure happens each morning, as Mesoké fills the celestial reservoir he will later use to give to his people. Mary always places a pot containing water at her holy places, so that Mesoké can fetch water any time he desires – for instance if it is cloudy or if he wants additional water. The rainbow that rises from the waterfalls like a python is a good and benevolent rainbow, since it fills the sky with water. By contrast, rainbows on dry land are bad and dangerous, since they empty the already dry land of water and moisture.

The rain-god Mesoké, the Itanda waterfalls, the rainbow and the python snakes complete the hydrological cycle. Even the rain-god must create rain, not by magic, but by literally filling heaven with physical water flowing in the river, which eventually will be returned to the catchment area and the river as rain. The force of the waterfalls testify to the immense powers of the rain-god and the python snake and the rainbow are links to heaven making the rains. The clouds need to be filled.[3]

After we had talked about Mesoké and the failing rains and harvests, and had discussed the fact that fewer and fewer people are paying their respects to Mesoké and the traditional cosmology, Mary had a suggestion. Not only was I interested in her water cosmology, with all the gods and spirits, but rain was also desperately needed. Therefore, Mary suggested, I should make a sacrifice of a goat to Mesoké to ensure that the good rains would come. It was difficult to disagree with Mary about the need for rain, and I was interested in her cosmology. So a sacrifice it would be.

It is obvious from an academic perspective that the sacrifice of a goat, even if the ritual is successful, cannot mitigate a meteorological drought. Leaving that to one side, however, it raises numerous questions about the role of tradition and of cultural and natural heritage in poverty alleviation, the constitution of society and future development. The main questions are:

- What is the role of cultural and natural heritage in debates about the causes of, the mitigation of and the solutions to poverty?

- What role do traditional and indigenous rituals and religions have in cultural and future heritage practices?

- How can culture, history and tradition be sources of development, and not merely be seen as a hindrance to modernization and prosperity?

While these questions are fairly broad, the aim is to address some aspects of these challenges by focusing on rainbows, pythons and waterfalls, since waterfalls are in many cases also part of the natural heritage. Thus, cultural and natural heritage combine at waterfalls, and ritual and religious practices (including intangible heritages) are not only part of a tangible heritage, but constitute a unity that links the past to the present and the future, and that links culture, nature and water.

Culture and poverty alleviation

In development discourse, the role of poverty and poverty mitigation has been discussed and debated for as long as development policies have existed and been implemented. In fact, since the dawn of civilization and religion, as the New Testament – and in particular Matthew 26:11 – testifies:

'The poor you will always have with you, but you will not always have me.'

If one follows this text, then, the solution to the problem of the poor is primarily a human matter, rather than a divine one.

Still, the role and importance of culture are rarely emphasized. The Sustainable Development Goals (SDG) Agenda 2030 sets the tone. Target 4 of SDG 11 Sustainable cities and communities – "Make cities inclusive, safe, resilient and sustainable" – does include aspects of cultural and natural heritage: Target 11.4 reads "Strengthen efforts to protect and safeguard the world's cultural and natural heritage."[4] The fact that the cultural and natural (sic) heritage is a sub-goal of sustainable cities suggests that it was by no means a main priority. Still, one must give credit to the decision and policy makers who included protecting and safeguarding cultural and natural heritage in this SDG target.

Intuitively, the role of cultural and natural heritage in poverty alleviation is obvious and important: heritage, cultural traditions and religious values are resources that span the past, present and future. Or put differently, they represent and constitute the profound realities of life that are themselves necessary for someone to be a complete human being. It is also from this perspective that cultural poverty can be approached, as UNESCO emphasizes: "Today it is widely held that one cannot consider only the economic part of poverty. Poverty is also social, political and cultural. Moreover, it is considered to undermine human rights … (the right to maintain one's cultural identity and be involved in a community's cultural life).'[5] And 'culture' is not something extra tacked onto society and economic development: 'The cultural sector provides a sustainable economic resource in which communities are empowered in their own economic development."[6] Thus,

> Placing culture at the heart of development policy constitutes an essential investment in the world's future and a pre-condition to successful globalization processes that take into account the principles of cultural diversity. It is UNESCO's mission to remind all States of this major issue. As demonstrated by the failure of certain projects underway since the 1970s, development is not synonymous with economic growth alone. It is a means to achieve a more satisfactory intellectual, emotional, moral and spiritual existence. As such, development is inseparable from culture … In this regard, the major challenge is to convince political decision-makers and local, national and international social actors to integrating the principles of cultural diversity and the values of cultural pluralism into all public policies, mechanisms and practices, particularly through public/private partnerships.[7]

Cultural heritage and poverty

Following UNESCO, cultural and natural heritage may encompass several categories of heritage:

Cultural heritage:
- Tangible cultural heritage:
    * movable cultural heritage (paintings, sculptures, coins, manuscripts)
    * immovable cultural heritage (monuments, archaeological sites, and so on)
    * underwater cultural heritage (shipwrecks, underwater ruins and cities)
- Intangible cultural heritage: oral traditions, performing arts, rituals

Natural heritage:
- natural sites with cultural aspects such as cultural landscapes, physical, biological or geological formations.[8]

Thus, the mythology of hydrology combines both cultural and natural heritage, since spectacular waterfalls are, or have the potential to be, natural heritage sites. The Itanda Falls, for instance, are included in the Indemnity Agreement protecting the falls as part of the construction of the Bujagali Dam and the destruction of the Bujagali Falls. The Indemnity Agreement of 2007 states that 'the obligations of Uganda under this Indemnity Agreement are irrevocable, absolute and unconditional' and says that Uganda shall 'set aside the Kalagala Falls Site exclusively to protect its natural habitat and environmental and spiritual values in conformity with sound social and environmental standards … Uganda also agrees that it will not develop power generation that could adversely affect the ability to maintain the above-stated protection at the Kalagala Site without the prior agreement by the Association.'[9] The Itanda Falls are a source of cultural and natural heritage, and the waterfalls are a spectacular site attracting many visitors from far away.

Without going into detail on the concepts of 'culture' and 'heritage', one may briefly point out a few aspects. 'Culture' has been debated ever since 1871, when the British anthropologist Edward Tylor defined it thus: 'Culture or Civilization, taken in its widest ethnographic sense, is that complex whole which includes knowledge, belief, art, morals, custom, and any other capabilities and habits acquired by man as a member of society.'[10] A century later, the 1982 Mexico Declaration defines culture as:

> … the whole complex of distinctive spiritual, material, intellectual and emotional features that characterize a society or social group. It includes not only the arts and letters, but also modes of life, the fundamental rights of the human being, value systems, traditions and beliefs… [culture] gives man the ability to reflect upon himself. It is culture that makes us specifically human, rational beings, endowed with a critical judgment and a sense of moral commitment. It is through culture that we discern values and make choices. It is through culture that man expresses himself, becomes aware of himself, recognizes his incompleteness, questions his own

achievements, seeks untiringly for new meanings and creates works through which he transcends his limitations.[11]

The fact that no cultures are static or represent a unit – culture aims to conceptualize lived lives – was also stressed by Herskovits as early as 1945:

> To think in terms of a single pattern for a single culture is to distort reality … for no culture is [so] simple [as not] to have various patterns. We may conceive of them as a series of interlocking behavior and thought and value systems, some even in conflict with others. The pattern of fundamental values in a society … will be effective over the entire group; but there will be subpatterns by which men order their lives differently from women, young and middle-aged folk from elders, members of lower from those of higher socioeconomic status … But all must be taken into account when an understanding of the mutations of culture in change is the end of the analysis.[12]

'Heritage' is also a wide, open resource for constructions of culture and identities, and it has multiple definitions that seek to capture specific cultural aspects; definitions of heritage are often quite similar to definitions of culture, for instance:

> 'Heritage' is everything that belongs to the distinct identity of a people and which is theirs to share, if they wish, with other peoples. It includes all of those things which international law regards as the creative production of human thought and craftsmanship, such as songs, stories, scientific knowledge and artworks. It also includes inheritances from the past and from nature, such as human remains, and naturally-occurring species of plants and animals with which a people has long been connected.[13]

At least from the perspectives of humanities, the importance of cultural and natural heritage goes without saying, and intuitively it makes sense beyond the sphere of humanities and practitioners such as archaeologists and anthropologists.

The concept and understanding of poverty also has a long and changing history.[14] Moreover, the relationship between poverty and culture is complex. For instance, the concept of 'cultural poverty' was introduced by Oscar Lewis in the late 1950s and early 1960s. Lewis argued that sustained poverty generates new sets of cultural practices, beliefs and attitudes that over time will maintain people in poverty.[15] Today, it could have been framed in terms of (for instance) Giddens' structuration theory,[16] but critics of Lewis claimed that this approach 'blamed the victims'.[17] Lewis himself was profoundly disturbed by the blame-the-victim interpretation: 'There is nothing in the concept that puts the onus of poverty on the character of the poor.'[18] However, a long debate ensued about whether one can explain people's poverty by their cultural values, and the original idea was abandoned. This is not the approach used here, where there is a focus on the role of heritage and water in the constitution of traditions and society. Culture is nevertheless essential in this process, as has been pointed out: 'Developing a more complete understanding of the conditions that produce and sustain poverty requires analysing empirically with greater detail and accuracy how the poor make sense of and explain their current conditions, options and decisions.'[19]

Thus, there has been a shift and culture is back on the agenda – also with regard to poverty studies; but the challenge is to conceptualize the role and importance of culture. An emphasis on heritage and tradition may help unravel this Gordian knot. It is obviously not about blaming the victims, but about placing emphasis on the role of culture in a broad and ontological sense, where it constitutes the social being and the self, whereby an individual can live a dignified life as a complete person, together with others. While not the theme of this study, the consequences of lost traditions and heritage are most likely subaltern people and groups, as the concept was originally developed by Gramsci – where some people lie outside the hegemonic power structures. These are not only political and geographical realities, but also social and cultural structures of domination and oppression.[20]

If one is a subsistence farmer dependent on the erratic and unpredictable life-giving rain, then water is inevitably a fundamental part of culture, society and religion. In an era of climate change, the consequences of failing rains and harvests may be even more poverty and deeper poverty traps that are almost impossible to escape.

The role of cultural heritage in Africa and elsewhere is part of the right of indigenous peoples to the past, territories, resources and futures. Given the limitations of this study and for the sake of simplicity, I will focus only on heritage here,[21] since it assigns a stronger role to traditions, ritual practices and religious beliefs, which in this case centre on rainbows, pythons, waterfalls – and rainmaking. Importantly, heritage is not something static that is inherited from the past: it is a living engagement and continuity of tradition that shapes the present and the future.

As has been pointed out:

> [H]umans walk into the future facing backwards … history provides a potent social weapon. People use history to posit themselves with respect to others: to entitle some individuals and to deny others rights to resources, citizenship, and social status … People without history are unable to identify themselves for others. Conversely, people use history to identify their common interests and to enter into effective political coalitions.[22]

Moreover, people are also religious and, as Barth argues, the most fruitful way to approach cosmology is to perceive it as 'a living tradition of knowledge – not as a set of abstract ideas enshrined in collective representations'.[23] From a religious perspective, religion is about the real reality, beyond and behind this visible and mundane world of everyday life and challenges. Thus, cosmology 'is not merely about a world out there, isolated from the self. More essentially, it provides a web of concepts, connections and identities whereby one's own attitudes and orientation to the various parts of the world are directed and moulded.'[24]

Water and religion as cultural and natural heritage

Religion is an interpretative concept, and people who label themselves religious do not need to agree what 'religion' is when they feel that they are religiously committed; but they actively take a stand on what they think religion should be, involving cosmic rules in this world and the world beyond. As Tim Insoll says regarding definitions of religion, religion is 'concerned with thoughts, beliefs, actions and material, and how these are weighted will vary; but in general terms, the simpler the definition the better'.[25] Religion is often the key building block of identity, and hence it 'can be conceived of as the superstructure into which all other aspects of life can be placed'.[26] Religion is also one of the key elements or forces shaping and defining tradition, and when traditions are founded in religions, they are often very conservative, representing social anchors in the past for solutions in the present and guidelines for the future.

The Oxford English Dictionary defines tradition thus: 'Tradition: the transmission of customs or beliefs from generation to generation, or the fact of being passed on in this way … a long-established custom or belief that has been passed on from one generation to another.'[27] The transmission of knowledge and heritage from generation to generation represents active engagements where values and social bonds and relations are built. Traditional ties are strong in Africa in general; but this is not, so to speak, because Africans are more 'traditional' than people elsewhere, but rather because these institutions are more necessary for social, cultural, political, economic and religious reasons. Moreover, for these traditional institutions to be fully active and ready for use, they must be renewed and modified through engagements and constant streams of social transactions, which include the ancestors.[28]

The role of religion may also be seen as part of lived history. As Oyebade writes with regard to African history and its social role:

> History was not an abstract concept. It was not a purposeless acquisition of knowledge of past and present events. Rather, history was relevant, having a purpose necessary for the survival of a community's traditions. History served primarily as a socializing agent, playing a role in day-to-day living … History, therefore, constituted the pivot of the socializing process. It was a means through which every person was educated in the codes of conduct of the society, in the norms, values, and ethics of the culture. It was through the knowledge of history that each community defined itself and its relationship to other communities.[29]

Yet, as has been pointed out in other contexts, literate societies tend to develop in directions different from non-literate societies;[30] and in non-literate societies, myths often have a fundamental role, which also has to be seen in relation to religion and symbolism. Moreover, although religion is often associated with theology, it is also about the social and to re-connect (Latin religio means 'binding together' (or 'bonds' or 'relations'), while socio indicates 'compassion'). The compassionate and social bonds bind each and everyone together in reciprocal relations, where the order of relations acquires legitimacy.[31]

The social aspect of religion will be stressed when analysing cultural heritage and poverty. As will be seen later, this was one of the aspects that Mary Itanda stressed. While she is an adherent believer as being a key ritual specialist in the cosmology, the role of religion probes to the core of society as a glue uniting the community and creating social bonds of relevance outside the domain of religion. From this perspective, religion is not above or behind history, but is part of the tradition of lived lives that have constituted people and societies for centuries, and hence this heritage is part of the solutions that the future can build on from the past.

The Nile is everything

In the Busoga Kingdom, there is a Lusoga proverb that 'The Nile is Wealth.'[32] The proverb captures the essence of water – and what water brings forth: wealth in all its forms. The modern city of Jinja, the second-largest city in Uganda, has the slogan 'Kiyira gives richness', meaning that the river gives everything. Jinja's municipal armorial bearings contain the same motto. In Luganda, the motto reads: Kiyira bwe bugagga. In 1963, the official presentation and interpretation of the emblem was (Figure 3):

Figure 3. Jinja's municipal armorial bearings (to the right) on a billboard at the source of the White Nile. Photo: Terje Oestigaard.

> The hippopotamus is representative of the fauna of the district. The rock, or stone,
> is a reference to the name Jinja which in Luganda means the stone and is thought
> to have historical significance. The wavy bar … denotes the river Nile at the source
> of which Jinja stands. The cotton plants refer to one of the principal crops of
> Busoga District in which Jinja is situated and the cogwheel and flash of lightning
> allude to industrial development and the Owen Falls Hydro-electric scheme on the
> Nile, which is the source of energy for the industry and the country in general.
> The group of a shield, spears, drums and an antelope's head is a representation of
> the badge used by the Busoga African Local Government.[33]

There can be no doubt that electricity, modernity and industrial development are important today and in the future, but the primary aim of this book is to focus on the other – often neglected – aspects of development: cultural and natural heritage, tangible and intangible heritage, and tradition, rituals and religions. The rain-god Mesoké, living as a river-god in the Itanda waterfalls, is an instructive case study, because it connects the hydrological cycle, rain, the python and the rainbow. And not least, it is still a living tradition – although it is declining, with fewer and fewer people believing in the indigenous and traditional religion.

Chapter 2 starts with a brief introduction to the science and studies of the rainbow. Since antiquity (and even before Aristotle), the rainbow and its colours have mesmerized humans and posed great challenges; and throughout the millennia most great thinkers and philosophers have been puzzled by the rainbow. Given that it has fascinated scientific minds since the dawn of history, it is no wonder that the rainbow has also been an important image in cosmologies – including as rainbow serpents.

Chapter 3 continues with an analysis of giant snakes and serpent-worship. Snakes, and in particular giant snakes, have always haunted and fascinated humans. Snakes are creatures with truly unique characteristics: they are life-givers and lethal at the same time, and throughout the world serpent-worship has been closely linked to fertility cults. Snakes in general – and pythons in particular – have been closely linked to the rainbow, and thus also connect the earthly and divine spheres.

Chapter 4 discusses some of the religious rainbows in history. From traditional and indigenous religions to world religions like Christianity, the rainbow has a prominent place in various cosmologies. As a natural phenomenon everywhere – though one that seldom appears – the rainbow has also had a central place in structural theories that aim to explain similarities across time, space and different cultures. The rainbow is most commonly linked with rainmaking and the forthcoming rain, and therefore it represents a totality unifying the cosmological and hydrological cycles.

Chapter 5 presents in depth the ethnographic documentation of the Busoga rainbow cosmology and the relation between rainmaking, the rainbow, the python, the waterfalls and sacrifices to the rain-god Mesoké. Mary Itanda's specific water-world along the Itanda waterfalls, with a particular emphasis on rain, forms the cosmology for the rainmaking sacrifice conducted to please the rain-god. And the chapter concludes with the outcome of the ritual when I visited Mary seven months later and the rain-god Mesoké decided to announce his presence in the most spectacular and convincing way.

Chapter 6 continues with an analysis of rainmaking practices in theory and reality, and why this ritual tradition has had a special historical role in African pasts. The variation in rain or the agro-water variability is larger in Africa than in most other parts of the world, making farmers extremely dependent on the highly unpredictable rains. With this as the background, there follows a discussion of water as an empirical, methodological and theoretical approach and the importance of understanding the role of water in history and societies, and in religions.

Chapter 7 concludes with a discussion of history and heritage and how cultural studies are important for the future. The history of historical and archaeological thoughts and studies in Africa has a troubled past, and by returning to the role of culture in poverty studies and the political processes of poverty alleviation, cultural heritage is emphasized as one important aspect of many others – often neglected, but still a fundamental part of the future.

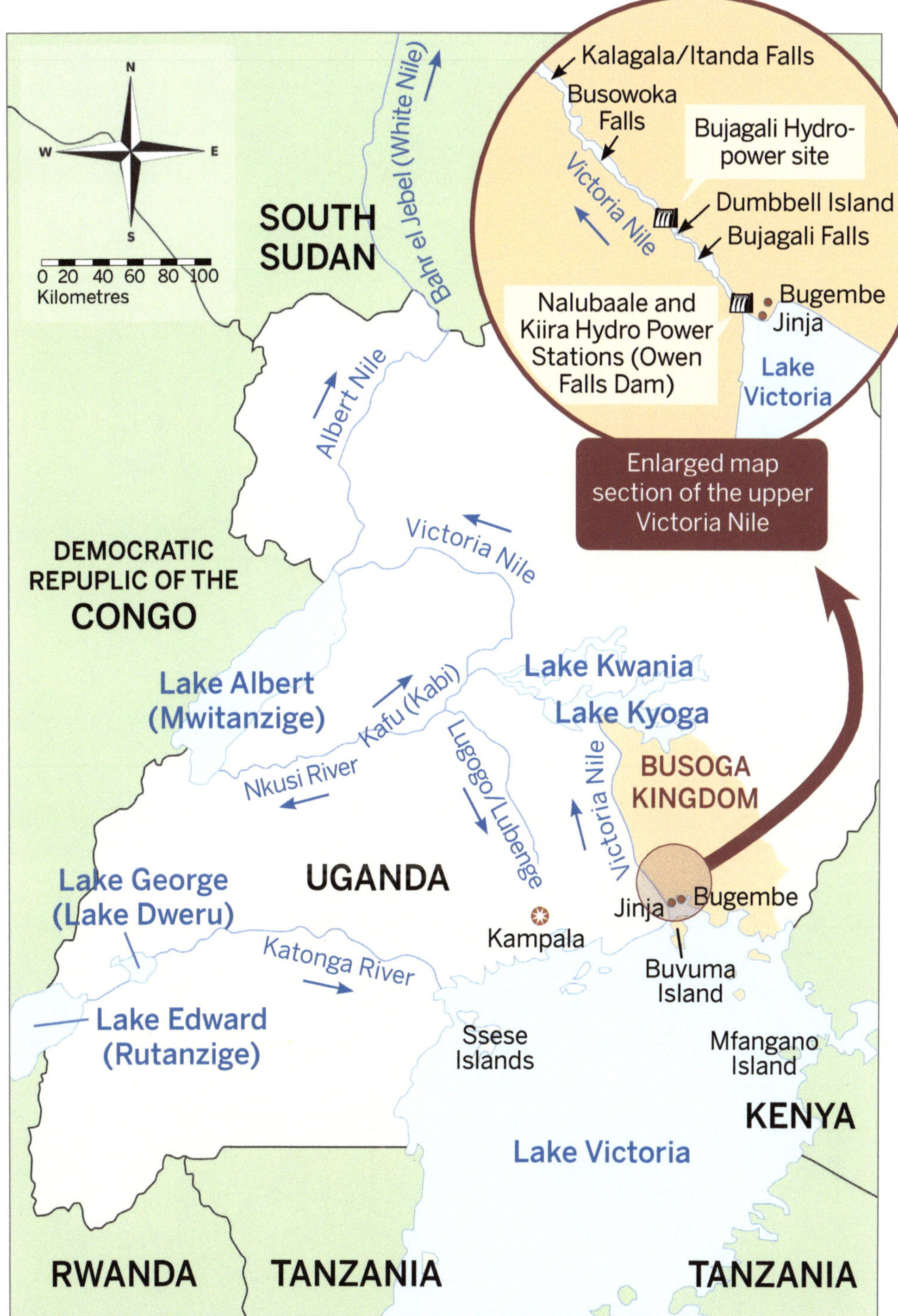

Figure 1b. Map of Uganda with waterfalls and dams. Made by Henrik Alfredsson, Nordic Africa Institute.

Photo: iStock (Rainbow over lake in Finland)

Chapter 2

Figure 4. Rainbow over Mui Ne, Vietnam. Photo: Terje Oestigaard.

2. Senses and science and rainbows

> Water –
> never blocks the light –
> Its ever moving skin
> radiates; its single vision parses into colors
> explicates what's embodied
> within light
>
> That rainbow
> water sketches on a blue slate
> is a disquisition –
> – what is and what is seen
> born forth in their fullness
> by light
>
> Purna Bahadur Vaidya, 'Water is water[34]

Mesmerizing humans

The rainbow is a unique mystery – a mundane happening and yet a rare experience (Figure 4). As the physicist Herch Nussenzveig wrote in 1977:

> When sunlight is scattered by raindrops, why is it that colorful arcs appear in certain regions of the sky? Answering this subtle question has required all the resources of mathematical physics … Some of the most powerful tools of mathematical physics were devised explicitly to deal with the problem of the rainbow and with closely related problems. Indeed, the rainbow has served as a touchstone for testing theories of optics. With the more successful of those theories it is now possible to describe the rainbow mathematically, that is, to predict the distribution of light in the sky.[35]

It is no wonder that the rainbow has a prominent place in religion and cosmology, when it has fascinated human minds throughout the ages and has also been a great philosophical puzzle since the days of Aristotle. One philosopher who struggled to understand the colours in the rainbow was René Descartes (1596–1650). He once said that 'the reason for the colors in the rainbow' caused him 'more trouble than all sublunary phenomena'. In his 'On the apparition of several suns', Descartes concludes: 'I hope that those who have understood everything that has been said in this treatise will in the future not see anything in the clouds whose cause they cannot easily understand, or anything that gives them subject for admiration.'[36]

Even Ludwig Wittgenstein devoted his last precious time on this earth to the puzzle of the rainbow. His final work *Remarks on Colour* was written during his trip to Vienna in 1950 and while he was dying of cancer in Cambridge.[37] The challenge he returned to in this small work was originally presented in his *Tractatus Philosophico-Mathematicus*, namely the logical structure of colour concepts. Wittgenstein asks: 'And is white simple, or does it consist of the colours of the rainbow?'[38] Wittgenstein called the colour problem a part of 'puzzle problems' or 'puzzle propositions'. The questions about colour – such as what makes bright colours bright and are 'pure' colours only abstractions and never found in reality? – probed to the core of philosophical understanding of the world, although Wittgenstein himself did not see his observations on colour as the pinnacle of his career.[39]

Wittgenstein's stand on colour straddled the divide between the followers of Isaac Newton (1642–1727) and Johann Wolfgang von Goethe (1749–1832). The term 'spectrum' (from the Latin *specere* – 'to look') was adopted by Sir Isaac Newton to describe and characterize the seven colours of the rainbow. According to Newton, there are seven primary colours in the spectrum, which match the seven notes on the musical scale – hence this was seen as confirmation of the divine harmony of nature.[40] However, this was not a scientific breakthrough. The most essential consequence of Newton's work was that colour theory was transferred from philosophy and painting to mathematics and optics. Since Aristotle (384–322 BCE), everyone had held that colours were properties of things and objects; Newton, on the other hand, established that colours are an illusion stemming from human responses of the visual apparatus to different emissions of light.

Newton was the first to appreciate the true origins of colours, and he extended Descartes' geometric theory of how to explain the rainbow's colours. Moreover, he was the first to realize that rays are not truly coloured and that colours in general, including the rainbow, are constructs of the human cortex.[41] Moreover, the reason we see different colours is that different rays of the spectrum have different refractions.[42] However,

> Like Goethe, people still find it hard to accept that transparent light somehow produces an array of colors, every one of which is darker than light itself. Newton told the Royal Society in 1672 that this apparent contradiction represents 'the oddest if not the most considerable detection which hath hitherto been made in the operations of Nature'.[43]

In his classic work from 1704, *Opticks*, Newton writes about the rainbow:

> This bow never appears but where it rains in the sun-shine, and may be made artificially by spouting up water which may break aloft, and scatter into drops, and fall down like rain. For the sun shining upon these drops certainly causes the bow to appear to a spectator in a due position to the rain and the sun. And hence

it is now agreed upon, that this bow is made by refraction of the sun's light in drops of falling rain.

Newton also explained why there are sometimes double bows:

> Thus shall there be made two bows of colours, an interior and stronger, by one reflexion in the drops, and an exterior and fainter by two; for the light becomes fainter by every reflexion. And their colours shall lie in order to one another, the red of both bows bordering upon the space … which is between the bows.[44]

Although Newton has been described as a scientist 'with his prism and silent face', *Opticks* represented something completely new. While Newton's *Principa* from 1687 was written in the language of dry mathematics and otherwise in Latin, *Opticks* was deliberately made accessible to a broader non-scientific community.[45] Epstein and Greenberg say:

> The rainbow image came to Newton laden with over two thousand years' burden of interpretations. When Newton definitively explained the phenomenon in his Opticks, nonscientists thought he had decomposed and reintegrated a symbol of great power, displacing a large portion of its meaning forever from the sacred realm into the profane. His explanations, to judge by the responses to it, reached beyond optics; it implied, for Newton's audience, a cosmology and a psychology. Before the philosopher's rainbow, there was God's.[46]

Still, despite Newton's revolutionary approaches to science, he also had a secret interest, namely alchemy and the pursuit of the philosopher's stone that would turn other metals into gold. This side of Newton was discovered only when, in 1936, John Maynard Keynes bought a collection of Newton's papers, which until then had been dismissed as uninteresting. As Keynes said in a 1942 lecture:

> Newton was not the first of the age of reason. He was the last of the magicians, the last of the Babylonians and Sumerians, the last great mind which looked out on the visible and intellectual world with the same eyes as those who began to build our intellectual inheritance rather less than ten thousand years ago … Isaac Newton, a posthumous child born with no father on Christmas Day 1642, was the last wonderchild to whom Magi could do sincere and appropriate homage.[47]

In his *Theory of Colours*, Goethe opposed Newton's theory, because it would reduce earth to a grey ball moving around in space, and Goethe wanted to restore the colours 'to the general dynamic flow of life and action which the present age loves to recognize in nature'. Strangely enough, although Goethe points out that some of the complex issues 'will be more conveniently treated in connection with appearance of the rainbow', he never returns to the rainbow (apart from in a few incidental observations and in a couple of letters).[48]

In similar vein, during a dinner on 28 December 1817, John Keats (1795–1821) agreed with Charles Lamb (1775–1834) that 'Newton had destroyed all the poetry of the rainbow, by reducing it to a prism'. At about the same time, the physiologist John Abernethy (1764–1831) lamented that the materialists of the 'sciences of life' were destroying all the poetry of the living.[49] John Keats wrote his poem 'Lamia' in 1819:[50]

> Do not all charms fly
> At the mere touch of cold philosophy?
> There was an awful rainbow once in heaven:
> We know her woof, her texture; she is given
> In the dull catalogue of common things.
> Philosophy will clip an Angel's wings,
> Conquer all mysteries by rule and line,
> Empty the haunted air, and gnomèd mine—
> Unweave a rainbow …

But is science (and the prism) destroying poetry and art? In 1998, Richard Dawkins published the book *Unweaving the Rainbow. Science, Delusion and the Appetite for Wonder* and his answer was 'no'. Rather the contrary: science and poetry could indeed learn from each other, although he warns of 'bad poetic science'.[51] Leaving that scientific debate, the rainbow's rays have without doubt also lit up other fields of inquiry far beyond water droplets in the sun – in fact, from time immemorial the rainbow has challenged scientific minds and enlightened religious beliefs.

Colours of rainbows: Challenging great minds

'Brilliant color was rare in the premodern world … Color therefore became endowed with immense symbolic significance, suggesting an actuality beyond reality', says Finlay.[52] The colours of the rainbow were in a unique position in this regard, not only because of their intensity and clarity, but also because of the enormous size and shape of the rainbow and (not least) the temporality and sudden appearances – and disappearances (Figure 5). But this could be a double-edged sword. The monastic reformer St Bernard of Clairvaux (1090–1153) regarded flamboyant hues as the temptations of the devil, who was throwing a cloak over God's creation: 'We are blinded by colours!' In similar vein, a Protestant minister in the sixteenth century complained about the idolization as an offence against God: 'Every man has fallen in love with himself … painted over with so many colours, stuft full of pride and envy …'[53]

While Roger Bacon's (c. 1214–1292) scientific view of the rainbow has been described as having presumably a retarding influence on the theoretical development of this natural phenomenon, he did point out the seemingly moving character of the rainbow. As a natural phenomenon, it is very human, individual and personal from a phenomenological view:

Figure 5. The rainbow in Sande, Vestfold, Norway. Photo: Terje Oestigaard.

> From this it is evident, as we learn by experience, that there are as many rainbows as observers. For if two people stand observing the rainbow in the north and one moves westward, the rainbow will move parallel to him; if the other observer moves eastward, the rainbow will move parallel to him, and if he stands still, the rainbow will remain stationary … It is evident, therefore, that there are as many rainbows as observers, from which it follows that two observers cannot see the same rainbow, although an inexperienced person does not comprehend this fact … each observer must see his own rainbow.[54]

The fact that nobody sees exactly the same rainbow was known and discussed; but another puzzling phenomenon was the presence of double rainbows. The so-called primary rainbow is often followed by an exterior concentric bow called a secondary rainbow. Even Aristotle referred to this secondary rainbow. The common explanation was that the second rainbow was a reflection of the primary one. And if two rainbows existed, then a natural question would be whether a third was possible and existed. Aristotle thought not: 'Three rainbows or more are not found because even the second is fainter, so that the third reflection can have no strength whatever and cannot reach the sun at all.' Still, the topic of multiple rainbows was much discussed among Scholastic philosophers in the thirteenth and fourteenth centuries, and based on commentaries on Aristotle's *Meteorologica*, interest in the rainbow seems never to have been greater than in the fourteenth century.[55]

Theodoric of Freiberg wrote *De iride* in the years around 1304 to 1310. Later it came to be seen as the 'complete explanation of the principal rainbow' and 'the explanation commonly attributed to De Dominis and to Descartes'.[56] Theodoric's ideas, overlooked for centuries, may be seen as identical to those of Descartes – and indeed very modern. Since the Hellenic Age of science, and in particular the philosophy and theory highlighted by Anaxagoras (c. 500–428 BCE), the idea that the rainbow was a reflection of solar rays had held sway. Anaxagoras believed that the rays were reflected from the concave water cloud, and this argument – further elaborated by Aristotle's geometry – was common scientific knowledge for almost two millennia. From this perspective, Theodoric proposed novel ideas. He discovered that the reflection of the rays occurs not from the external convex surface of the drops, as Vitello – a thirteenth century scholar from the University of Padua – believed, but at the inner concave rear surface, where the solar rays are refracted. As Theodoric wrote:

> Let the radiation enter the oft-mentioned transparent body and pass through it to the opposite surface and from that be reflected internally back to the first surface by which it originally entered, and then after passing out let it go to the eye; such radiation, inasmuch as it is produced by a transparent spherical body, serves to explain the production of the rainbow.[57]

Scientifically, from a physical point of view, refraction is a process where light bends when it crosses an interface – like the one between the air through which the light is travelling freely and the surface of a raindrop. Refraction occurs together with dispersion.

White light is physically light of colours with different wavelengths. When the light crosses the boundary of a waterdrop, for instance, the various wavelengths are bent at different angles and dispersed. Hence, the different colours become visible and dispersion is an inevitable part of the rainbow.[58] This was a great discovery – the rays are refracted within the water droplet; but one is equally impressed by the philosophers in antiquity emphasizing the sun's reflection on the droplet's surface or outside.

Re-creating God's creation?

In Greek and Roman art, Iris is sometimes crowned with the rainbow. As the centuries of Christianity roll by, her appearance seems to change and she looks more like a Biblical angel. Originally, Iris was a lesser deity in the Greco-Roman pantheon and she had many names, characteristics and associated qualities: 'Rose-lipped Iris, daughter of Thaumas', 'Iris glided down to earth along her many-coloured bow' and 'Soaring to heaven on balanced wings, [Iris] blazed a rainbow trail beneath the clouds as she flew … Iris, glory of the sky, cloud-borne.'[59] She was also associated with romance.

The rainbow has been central to understanding colours in general, and in nature in particular. Leonardo da Vinci (1452–1519) in his *Trattato della pittura* (*A Treatise on Painting*) also referred to the rainbow's colours as the natural manifestation and harmony of colours.[60] The materiality of the Renaissance garden played a central role in the development of Cartesian mechanical and mathematical philosophy; the mechanical human body and the immaterial mind. Descartes has been seen as a man who 'preferred understanding to admiration', and therefore aimed to use mathematics to explain the rainbow so that there would no longer be any occasion to wonder at this admirable display. The artificial rainbow fountain had a crucial role to play here. Originally coming from Renaissance Italy, the rainbow fountain was a commonplace spectacle in palatial gardens in the sixteenth and seventeenth centuries throughout Europe. Usually it was a fine spray upwards or a downward cascade of water creating a rainbow if the observer stood with the sun behind him or her. 'Descartes reconfigured traditional boundaries of art and nature, wonder and skill, to make a description of the rainbow using the fountain as a basis for his explanation', says Werrett.

> In doing so, traditional distinctions between art and nature were broken down – art, the mechanism of the fountain, became the source of the description of nature. The consequences of this reconfiguration, finally, are assimilated into Cartesian divisions of mind and body, reason and artisanal labour.[61]

Thus, making a rainbow has profound implications for the understanding of the divide between mind and matter, culture and nature – and indeed God and humans:

> The creation of artificial rainbows accorded with Renaissance Neoplatonist belief that humans were capable of imitating or even superseding Nature through artifice,

since Nature herself was only imitating a higher, spiritual sphere. Designers spoke of cultivating and improving nature through artifice to create a new, higher form, a 'third nature' which blended both nature and art.[62]

The rainbow fountains were also contemporary entertainment invoking playfulness, wonders and surprises; the rainbows were so real that many would not believe that they were made mechanically.

> This conception of a playful Nature and the human ability to cultivate her through art provided the raison d'être of the Renaissance garden. The garden became a microcosm, an imitation and improvement of Nature, containing 'all the delights that were scattered throughout the universe' according to Colonna.[63]

Mechanics had a very pedagogical role as well. The fountain engineers' wonders were not really different from other tricks, and wonders became a resource. The artificial rainbow was perfect as an example for Descartes to illustrate his ideas and methods:

> After drawing attention to the works of men in things corporeal, after having stirred wonder in you by exhibiting to you the machines, extremely powerful, very strange and rare automata, visual appearances seemingly real and impostures the subtlest that artificers can devise, I will then uncover the secret devices on which they rest and these are so simple that you will no longer be tempted to feel wonder regarding any product of human devising. I shall then pass on to the works of nature.[64]

Although they were made artificially in the rainbow fountains, Descartes regarded all these rainbows as wholly natural. He compared the human-made rainbows to the natural ones and ascribed to them the same causes:

> Considering that this bow appears not only in the sky, but also in the air near us, wherever there are drops of water illuminated by the sun, as we see in certain fountains, I readily decided that it arose only from the way in which the rays of light act on these drops and pass from them to our eyes.[65]

Thus, Descartes' conclusion was clear: it was the sun and light, not men, creating rainbows – in other words, nature not culture.

> Descartes's rejection of the distinction between 'artificial' and 'natural' rainbows was not simply a challenge to Aristotelian traditions ... Since Descartes rejected the Renaissance idea of cultivating a phenomenon through art distinct from the natural, the thought behind the 'artificial' rainbow, he instead proposed an alternative wonder based not on transforming but manipulating Nature.[66]

According to himself, Descartes made 10,000 observations of the rainbow's rays striking the upper half of the globe. He calculated that the radius of the rainbow is 42° – or more precisely, he estimated the greatest radius at 41°47' and the smallest at about 40°. Still, few scientists have been accused of plagiarism as often as Descartes, and the 42° radius seems to have been a well-established fact at least as far back as Vitello's *Opticae*, written between 1270 and 1278. Vitello wrote: 'some have observed that the height of the bow and the sun are together always just 42°', indicating that this figure did not originate with him; and Roger Bacon in his *Opus majus* from 1269 estimated that the maximum elevation of the rainbow was just 42°.[67] Also the rainbow disappears as a natural phenomenon when the sun rises beyond 42° in the sky.[68]

The rainbow: From science to religion

In the history of science and ideas,

> The rainbow had been a central problem of science from the time of Aristotle's work on meteorology – his study of all things below the moon – through the work of Newton in 1669–1671, or to carry the story further, until the work of the happily named British scientist George Airy, who in the mid-nineteenth century made the last important synthesis within the theory of the rainbow.[69]

However, rainbows are not only about science, but also about aesthetics. As George Sarton said of some of the ancient Greek scholars: 'Men of science might accept the myths as poetical descriptions of things that were not susceptible of scientific explanation.'[70] And as Philip Fisher emphasizes, we realize that when we speak about the Seven Wonders of the World, the wonders are in relation to the visible world. The wonders are not only visual, but in order to become wonders, they must be unexpected or rare experiences. What appears to contradict water's normal behaviour in nature represents something beyond the everyday world.[71] Moreover, Fisher says,

> This act of striking us makes up the figure-ground relation itself, as an active fact. The sudden appearance of the rainbow, its rareness, its beauty are all part of this initial act of striking us, trapping and holding our attention by means of beauty and the unwilled response of wonder.[72]

Hence, 'the rainbow is, in every individual life, a rare experience, and it is always a sudden and an unexpected one … the rainbow could be taken as an epitome of an aesthetic experience'.[73] Moreover, the rainbow connects heaven and earth – either going from earth to heaven or the other way around, which is evident in the very name itself: 'If most people were asked what the rainbow's most characteristic feature is, they would answer "the colours," but even the name of the phenomenon belies this response.

The most characteristic feature of the rainbow is its shape; it is a bow, or portion of a circle.'[74] It is therefore a divine link to heaven connecting the different realms.

Despite all scientific explanations, the rainbow has always been something else, something bigger and different; and if there is one natural phenomenon in the world that can serve as a cultural and religious symbol, it is the rainbow. But before turning to religious rainbows, one should focus on giant snakes, pythons and serpent cosmologies, since these are often seen as identical or parallel to the rainbow and as connecting the different realms.

"Despite all scientific explanations, the rainbow has always been something else, something bigger and different; and if there is one natural phenomenon in the world that can serve as a cultural and religious symbol, it is the rainbow."

Photo: Terje Oestigaard

Chapter 3

Figure 6. Reticulated python, Taronga Zoo, Sydney. Photo: Terje Oestigaard.

3. Giant snakes and rainbow serpents

'Basically, the life of a snake is cyclic: feeding, digesting, shedding, and hibernating or estivating.'[75]

'Snakes arouse more extreme emotions in man than does any other type of animal. Much of the emotion is unreasoning fear – fear often so overpowering that it produces shock … A vast superstructure of imagination has been built around snakes, and it has reached incredible proportions in the forms of myths, folklore, tall tales, and misconceptions of size, shape and habits.'[76]

The giants: fact and fiction

From time immemorial, rumours and stories about gigantic snakes have flourished, with some more extraordinary and fantastic than others. According to Roman sources, a 120-foot-long [ca. 36 m] snake was found in Africa along the Bagradas River. Livy in the first century BC was one of the main authors, although the best detailed account is preserved by Orosius (c. AD 385–420):

> Regulus, chosen by lot for the Carthaginian War, marched with his army to a point not far from the Bagradas River and there pitched his camp. In that place a reptile of astonishing size devoured many of the soldiers as they went down to the river to get water. Regulus set out with his army to attack the reptile. Neither the javelins they hurled nor the darts they rained upon its back had any effect … Finally, when Regulus saw that it was sidelining a great number of his soldiers with its bites, was trampling them down by its charge, and driving them mad by its poisonous breath, he ordered ballistae brought up. A stone taken from a wall was hurled by a ballista; this struck the spine of the serpent and weakened the constitution of its entire body … Hence this serpent, which had for a long time withstood so many javelins unharmed, moved about disabled from the blow of a single stone and, quickly overcome by spears, was easily destroyed. Its skin was brought to Rome – it is said to have been one hundred and twenty feet in length – and for some time was an object of wonder to all.[77]

Supersnakes of enormous size have, throughout history, been central to myths and alleged observations. An enormous snake in Uganda was reported to Captain Pitman in the 1930s. This snake was allegedly 130 feet long [ca. 40 m], but nobody got the skin after its death to document this. The animal was buried, but apparently during the night three locals dug out the buried snake and ate it all, which is quite an achievement, given that the weight would have been thousands of pounds. Elsewhere, for instance in the Philippines, 50-foot-long [ca. 15 m] pythons have been reported, and throughout history from ancient times, supersnakes have been documented. Rumours apart, the snake skins have often been used as an indicator and measurement of the size of the serpents. In the case of one snake, its flesh was measured at 2,180 mm, but when the skin was dried and stretched it measured 2,650 mm. In other words, the skin was over 20 per cent longer than the original length of the snake.[78]

Clifford Pope notes three ways of determining the size of a snake:

> The first is strictly scientific, which demands concrete proof and therefore may err on the conservative side by waiting for evidence in flesh. This approach rejects virtually all field measurements. The next level attempts to weigh varied evidence and come to a balanced, sensible conclusion; field measurements by experienced explorers are not rejected, and even reports of a less scientific nature are duly evaluated. The third level leans on a belief that a lot of smoke means some fire.[79]

In the world of reptiles, the world's longest snake has always fascinated and haunted human imagination, and there is something magical and mythological about 10 metres or 33 feet. However, many herpetologists are sceptical about whether snakes have ever reached such gigantic lengths, and 10 metres is somehow a theoretical maximum length that many scholars are willing to accept. The field measurements of such snakes are, however, dubious, although even the *Guinness Book of World Records* 1991 seems to have accepted a *Python reticulatus* measuring 33 feet. The largest African rock python (*Python sebae*) ever documented seems to have been a 9.8 metre (32 feet) snake killed in 1932 in the Ivory Coast, although here, too, full details are lacking and thus the size cannot be verified. In 1927, the famous English herpetologist Arthur Loveridge measured the fresh skin of a python from Lake Victoria at 9.1 metres; even allowing for extensive stretching, its length must have been more than 7 metres. From West Africa, another skin was measured at 9.1 metres. Thus, there might have been giants of 9 metres in the past, and perhaps some exist even today. However, it is highly unusual to find species longer than 5 metres nowadays, and the average length of adults is 3–4 metres.[80]

Globally, there are four species of giant snakes commonly reported to exceed 20 feet in length: the common (or green) anaconda (*Eunectes murinus*), the African (or rock) python (*Python sebae*), the Indian (including Burmese) python (*Python molurus*) and the reticulated python (*Python reticulatus*).[81] The boa constrictor can reach 18–19 feet. The amethystine or scrub python is said to reach at least 22 feet, but little is known about it.[82]

A Brazilian herpetologist has argued that the anaconda's maximum length is 12–13 metres (39–42 feet) or perhaps 14 metres (slightly less than 46 feet). A more reliable although not proven measurement is a 37.5-foot-long anaconda, and many will give the anaconda as a species the maximum length of 30 feet to be on the safe side. The maximum length of the African rock python is generally accepted to be 25 feet.[83]

Whether the anaconda or the reticulated python is the longest in the world is disputed and unsettled, although more reports favour the anaconda (perhaps because the python is slenderer) (Figure 6): if a 20-foot reticulated python and a 20-foot anaconda were placed side by side, most people would regard the anaconda as bigger because of its bulk. And herein lies part of the challenge with giant snakes – and even with the belief in supersnakes: they appear bigger than they actually are. Since these giants are mesmerizing and unbelievable creatures, in particular while swimming, they may seem much larger monsters than they actually are. In Brazil, for instance, an anaconda was observed swimming down the river. It appeared to be 40 feet long, but was actually around 20. Another account comes from a medical doctor who saw an anaconda by moonlight and felt sure it was 30 feet long; when killed, the snake turned out to be 19 feet in length and 14 inches in diameter.[84] In practice, it is impossible to estimate the size of a giant snake with any accuracy because they are so impressive and spectacular that they become giants whether in the water, on land or in trees.

Snakes – creatures without arms or legs – move in striking ways, and sometimes at high speed. The most common is a sideways wave-like motion. Sometimes there is not enough space and they need to advance in a straight line: that is also possible, since snakes can use their belly skin to slither straight ahead.[85]

The African rock python, in particular, uses a combination of aquatic and arboreal ambush sites. In bodies of water, serpents can lie submerged for long periods of time with only their eyes and nostrils exposed. From this position, they attack animals coming to drink. However, they are also excellent climbers: they can lie in wait on tree branches and then silently drop down on their prey passing below.[86]

The python possesses immense strength: they have been reported to have killed leopards, as well as crocodiles. And when it comes to the size of their prey, giant snakes are remarkable. There is at least one authenticated case where a 37 kilogram *Python sebae* killed a 35 kilogram impala and started swallowing it: thus adult snakes can handle animals with 95 per cent of their own body weight. Actually, this is a conservative figure, since pit vipers have been documented eating prey equal to 160 per cent of their own body weight. Since the weight of some of the largest anacondas may exceed 135 kilograms, they can clearly swallow some very big animals. Given the size of their prey, these giant reptiles do not need to eat very often. One of the longest fasts recorded for any giant snake featured an anaconda that lived in confinement for three years without eating anything. An Indian python has been reported to have gone without food for 30 months and an African python for 33 months. However, it seems that many of these extremely long fasts are related to captivity, and the snakes refuse to eat even when they are given the chance.[87]

Pythons may also eat humans, and a missionary magazine offered some advice to those working in Africa on how to react if they were attacked by a python:[88]

> Remember not to run away, the python can move faster. The thing to do is to lie flat on the ground on your back with your feet together, arms to the sides and head well down. The python will then try to push its head under you, experimenting at every possible point. Keep calm, one wiggle and he will get under you, wrap coils round you and crush you to death. After a time the python will get tired of this and will probably decide to swallow you without the usual preliminaries.

> He will very likely begin with one of your feet. Keep calm. You must let him
> swallow your foot. It is quite painless and will take a long time. If you lose your
> head and struggle he will quickly whip his coils around you. If you keep calm,
> he will go on swallowing. Wait patiently until he has swallowed about up to your
> knee. Then carefully take out your knife and insert it into the distended side of his
> mouth and with a quick rip slit him up.

Although this probably is a good technique if attacked, humans are not the pythons'
preferred prey. However, giant snakes – and, in Africa particularly pythons – have an
important and omnipotent role in many cosmologies: 'Nowhere else on earth has the
giant snake in the flesh been elevated to the exalted position that it enjoyed from one
side to the other of this continent [Africa]. There can be little doubt that the African
rock python was the species most widely worshipped.'[89]

As real and mythological creatures, there is no doubt that snakes are believed to
possess extraordinary powers. As Murphy and Henderson wrote:

> There is no evidence that any snake has the ability to charm prey, but what most
> observers are actually seeing is the innate defense behavior of many animals to
> 'freeze' when confronted with a predator. However, this may not work very well
> with snakes because they are also using chemosensory and heat sensing abilities to
> locate their prey, and the prey animals may use the behavior at inappropriate times
> … Thus, 'freezing' in the presence of a snake may very well work to the prey's
> disadvantage when confronted by a snake.[90]

Snake and python worship

As pointed out, 'Because of their shape and their relation to the environment, snakes
play an important role in the beliefs of various people. Their swiftness and peculiar
locomotion, along with periodical sloughing of their skin, their glistening beauty, and
the venom of some species have given them a place apart in the animal world.'[91] The
popular fascination with the size of giant pythons goes far back into history, and whenever one of these giants is spotted, it receives a lot of attention.[92] Thus, 'in important
myths like those of creation, cosmogony, and fertility, the serpent's hold over thought
in ancient civilizations is remarkable'.[93]

One of the earliest studies of python worship is perhaps the account given by Willem
Bosman in his *Description of the Gulf of Guinea* (1705). With regards to the Whydah
snake worshippers, he says: 'Their principal god is a certain sort of snake which professes
the chief rank among their gods. They esteem the serpent their extreme good and general
bliss.'[94] Later accounts confirmed this picture, and the penalty for accidentally killing
a python was death (indeed, even just meeting the creature would result in a fine).
Apparently, any offender was burnt and there was no possibility of appeal. Indeed, it is
probable that even the king's power would have failed to protect someone who injured

Figure 7. Centralian carpet python, Taronga Zoo, Sydney. Photo: Terje Oestigaard.

the reptile from the people's fury.[95] The python was highly regarded and venerated, and it contained the spirit of a god of wisdom, bliss and benefaction. In times of drought (or excessive rainfall), snakes were involved, and it seems that at such times processions to the temple would take place.[96]

Snakes are particular and peculiar creatures with specific features unlike other animals (Figure 7). The reptiles move quickly and noiselessly, seemingly appearing from nowhere. They often live near graves, hollow trees, old walls and wells, and anthills. While pythons have enormous size and crushing power, other snakes are extremely poisonous and seem magical. Their forked tongues dart and their skins are often iridescent in colour. Snakes hatch large broods and pythons lay many eggs; all male snakes have two penises, and some even have four. Snakes may hibernate during cold and drought; then they reappear with the seasonal rains. And they swim in water. Hence, rainbows, rainmaking, fecundity and phallicism are within the natural realm of snakes' symbolic lives and appearances.[97] As predators, they are also different from other hunters, since they are 'gape limited': their prey is consumed completely and whole, and hence the gape of the jaws sets the limit on the size of the prey.[98]

Despite the immense strength of pythons, when facing humans they tend to move away deliberately or stay motionless, unless they are seriously harassed or threatened.[99] Apart from their huge size, pythons are also believed to have bizarre features. Thus, the python on an island in Lake Victoria 'comes roaring like an engine, and its presence is noticed by water foaming all over its path'.[100] Among one group in Malaysia,

> it is also believed that the rainbow-serpent is of such enormous size that it extends down to the regions of the underworld, from where it draws the waters to the surface of the earth. The light drizzling rain that falls when a rainbow is visible, is thought to be the sweat of the reptile; if this sweat happens to fall upon anyone who is not protected by a special amulet it causes a particular kind of sickness.[101]

Among the inhabitants of the Andaman Islands, the evil significance of the rainbow is a general feature, and in the rainbow they see sickness or death approaching one of their people.[102]

From one perspective, rain is semen and death is birth. 'A snake may cause harm and even death by its poison … In rain-making or rain-control the snake, or water serpent, is often the animal that brings rain, hence it brings fertility and life. It will transform at will and often have both these malevolent and benevolent aspects.'[103] In Brazil, among the Botocudo, there are beliefs that the great snake is the lord of waters which signals to the rain and makes it fall; the rainbow is called 'the urine of the great snake'. Among the Canella of eastern Brazil, it was believed that the rainbow's ends rested in the open mouths of two anacondas.[104] This is a theme in many cultures and cosmologies:

> The rainbow, visualized as 'celestial serpent', plays an important role not only in the mythology of African Pygmies, but also in their entire religious life. It is regarded as the magical, terror-inspiring, man-murdering snake monster that devours human beings and brings about catastrophes.[105]

That snakes are connected to other types of monsters is quite a common phenomenon, which again relates to the rainbow.

Dragons and rainbow serpents

In Chinese mythology, there is a belief that a serpent or dragon lives above the clouds to give rain; and similar myths are found in ancient India, where Vritra or Ahi is a throttling snake or dragon with three heads concealing the rain-clouds; it is therefore slain by Indra, who is also the beneficent giver of rain. In the Hebrew tradition, snakes are ascribed wisdom, and Greek diviners connected them with knowledge. Serpents were also a symbol of healing, and together with wisdom and life it includes the life-giving waters in the form of rain.[106]

In China, bronze mirrors have traditionally been invested with the power to avert calamities. In the *Eulogy on the Water Mirror* by Jia Zeng (d. 727), the 'coiling dragon residing in it' and the synergy with water are praised.

> The dragon image is always associated with, among other things, the efficacy of invoking rains. Daoist scriptures and ritual practices convey the conviction that the dragon pictures (longwen) and prayer can call forth dragons who dive into the four seas to bring waters to the drought-inflicted area.[107]

The 'curving rainbow' was used metaphorically to describe a dragon in a verse by the poet Ssu-ma Hsiang-ju (d. 117 BC),[108] and 'when drought afflicts the land [in China], the Dragon is besought to send down the needful rain, and in the due course does so'.[109] Moreover, the rain can be sexed and can symbolize fertility and procreation. The twelfth century BC Chinese I Ching hints of sexual duality when it says: 'The rainbow is the combination of yin and yang', which are the opposite and complementary female and male qualities contained in all life.[110]

Beliefs in dragons are so prevalent in many cultures and traditions and C.G. Jung suggested that dragons are 'archetypes'. 'Archetypes' are meant to designate the formal aspects of instincts, which 'express themselves in the form of unreflected, involuntary fantasy images, attitudes, and actions, which bear an inner resemblance to one another and yet are identical with the instinctive reactions specific of Homo sapiens'.[111] Jung himself resists the criticism that archetypes are inherited representations,[112] but archetypes are more to be seen as a structural condition of the psyche.[113] Still, as Robert Blust asks: why are dragons often associated with waterfalls, pools and caves? And why are dragons also widely seen as controllers of rain, and also portrayed as snakes? After a lengthy and cross-cultural analysis of dragons in Europe, the Near East (including Egypt), India, the Far East, Mesoamerica and North America, his thesis – put simply – is that dragons are the last stage of conceptual developments, which started with the rainbow.[114]

Following one of the most prominent draconologists, 'No dragon exists – none ever did exist.'[115] The rainbow serpent is in a middle position. The rainbow is usually represented in one of four ways: as a giant snake, as a celestial bow, as a bridge between heaven or earth, or as the apparel of a deity, like a belt or a scarf. 'By far the most common view is that the rainbow is a giant snake which either drinks water from the earth and sprays it over the sky (thus causing it to rain), or that drinks rain from the sky (thus causing it to stop).'[116] The notion and process whereby the rainbow drinks the water in heaven or the sky and thus stops the rain is found – inter alia – among the Muria of eastern India. In Chinese folk beliefs of Lanzhou in Gansu province, for instance, 'the rainbow is an enormous dragon which drinks water from the sea and sprays it out as rain'.[117]

Dragons share many of the same qualities and processes as rainbows – as signs of fertility and blessing, or as signs of drought or flooding. The genuine ambivalence and the rainbow as an evanescent phenomenon and as a snake causes a logical problem: when the sun and the rain battle for control of the sky, the serpent-rainbow is visible; but where is it at other times? The celestial snake is often described as rising or descending from a cave, spring, lake or river. Thus, the rainbow seems to have a celestial and a terrestrial appearance; a visible form in the sky and an invisible and aquatic form on earth.[118] Many others have argued that dragons are basically snakes in a different form. According to Blust:

> The rainbow is a weather phenomenon, and so does not exist in isolation. Since it can appear only when there is a conjunction of sun and rain it is closely associated with both fire and water. But rain comes in storms, and storms are accompanied by thunder and lightning.

These are also characteristics of dragons:

> In hindsight it is astonishing that the identity of the rainbow and the dragon has gone so long unrecognized. The clues are literally everywhere, once we abandon the idea that dragons are arbitrary creations of the human mind … like many other creations of traditional cultures, dragons are largely explicable as products of rational prescientific speculation about the world of real events, in this case the natural mechanism governing rainfall and drought.[119]

The rainbow-serpent myth complex

The rainbow serpent – and its associated cosmology – has had a central place in Aboriginal Australia. As Eliade noted, 'The Rainbow Snake is no more a rainbow than a snake. The "natural" meteorological phenomenon and the "natural" reptilian species are religiously valuable because they are related to a religious structure, that of the Rainbow Snake.'[120] Moreover,

> The Australian rainbow serpent is a mythic being of the Dreaming, the legendary Aboriginal time that began with the world's creation and that has no end. People, animals, and eternal beings like the Rainbow Serpent are all part of the Dreaming, and everyday life is affected by the Dreaming's immortals.[121]

Radcliffe-Brown was the first to identify the rainbow-serpent myth complex and its association with water in Australia (Figure 8). As he writes: 'There is found in widely separated parts of Australia a belief in a huge serpent which lives in certain pools or water-holes. This serpent is associated, and sometimes identified, with the rainbow.'[122] He continues:

> The association of the serpent with rain and rainmaking follows immediately from this central core … Those few places in which the water never entirely disappears may quite justifiably be regarded as being the permanent dwelling-place of the spirit of water as represented by the rainbow-serpent.[123]

Among the Feranmin people along Papua New Guinea's Upper Sepik River and its headwaters, the rainbow serpent is present in bodies of stagnant water. He causes thunderstorms when he is aroused, but ordinary rain when he is active and people are careful. The falling raindrops are the urine or the tears of the rainbow serpent, whose name is Magalim.[124]

Rock-art may also have represented immanent powers and capacities, as is evident from a rock-painting of a rainbow snake in Northern Kimberley: '[If] touched by a boy it will rain too much', since super-human beings were residing in caves.[125] In other words, the ancestors and divinities could penalize any deviation from social norms and any transgression of taboos with consequences and implications in the water-world – for instance, with too much or too little rain.

The X-ray style of rock-art was mainly produced between 1,400 and 3,000 years ago, but some forms may be as old as 6,000 or even 8,000 years. More recent rock-art usually contains the colours red, yellow, white and purple (the predominant colours), though orange, pink and black also occur. According to Taçon,

> It is combinations of colour in and around anatomical features that are most impor-tant for conveying abstract ideas related to the art, such as Dreamtime beliefs, conveying … Ancestral power through the use of bright combinations of pigment … This adds iridescence, likened to rainbows and Rainbow Serpents, as well as 'brightness', associated with other Ancestral Beings, to the images.[126]

The colours had an active and immanent power: 'Painting some creatures with brilliant "rainbow" colour thus enabled Aborigines to tap into the Ancestral force believed to be inherent in the landscape.'[127]

Tools were also closely associated and related to ancestral powers – in particular quartz and quartzite tools, which sometimes shimmer with bright reflected light. 'Brightness' or iridescence is a quality of life and ancestral beings, and 'this attribute makes rain-bows and Rainbow Serpents extremely potent as natural and supernatural phenomena,

Figure 8. Olive python, Taronga Zoo, Sydney. Photo: Terje Oestigaard.

for instance, and is one of the reasons quartz is often associated with medicine men, Rainbow Serpents and sacred rituals'.[128] By painting at quartzite sites, it was possible to tap into the powers of the ancestral beings, and 'in order to tap into the ultimate life-giving powers of Ancestral Beings it was necessary for Aborigines to unite male and female together, as with sexual intercourse. Much of this, for instance, is central to the Rainbow Serpent mythology of Western Arnhem land and beyond.'[129]

The Rainbow Serpent is not only one of the most powerful and widespread ancestral beings, but is central to oral history, ritual performance and visual art. Rock-painting of the Rainbow Serpent is found all over Australia, but in Arnhem Land there is a particularly large concentration, and the origin of these beliefs seems to go back 6,000 years.[130]

The rainbow has a very peculiar appearance and highly specific powers and associations. As Taçon, Wilson and Chippindale write:

> [H]igh up in the sky, sometimes before, sometimes after a storm, there appears a great serpent-like form full of elemental colour. A rainbow is born and soon more rainbows appear and travel across the land, heralding at once both great acts of creativity and destruction. Change is literally in the air. Old landscapes are destroyed while new ones are born. Every living creature is somehow affected.[131]

Thus, the occurrence of rainbows in dry areas where there is generally little rain is even more spectacular, because it is literally lighting up the world from nowhere. While the phenomenon is natural, it seems also to be unnatural – not only because of the illuminating colours, but also because of the scale of the phenomenon and its rarity. As such, the unnatural natural has often been ascribed supernatural qualities or divine powers. The gods manifest themselves in nature and through nature, but they are always gods superior and apart from the materiality that they choose to manifest themselves through for humans to comprehend and experience the divine presence.[132]

Among the Kunwinjku of Western Arnhem Land, the 'rainbow' is used to describe different distinct mythological themes. One is Yingarna, who is seen as the original creator being or the 'first mother' of all things. In some myths, Yingarna's first born is a male rainbow. Rainbow serpents are often androgynous or bisexual in various degrees, and hence also related to seasonal fertility through the life-giving rains.[133]

In recent years, the rainbow serpent has gained an iconic status, symbolizing Aboriginal spirituality in numerous ways (for better or worse), including through New Age books and beliefs.[134] One of the largest rainbow serpents documented in rock-art is an enormous red-and-yellow serpent at Lilydale Spring, among the Waanyi, measuring 5.8 metres in length and 2.8 metres in height.[135]

The rock art itself also has the immanent capacity to boost powers:

> When the aborigines want to increase the supply of water-snakes in the lagoons they choose the correct season, and standing before the painting, beat it lightly with a bough to hunt out the spirits of the water-snake, directing them meanwhile

to go to the various waterholes and there become large water-snakes. By means of this simple magical formula the aborigines believe that there will be an adequate food supply.[136]

The sites associated with the rainbow snake are also seen as sources of fertility power and ideas related to the recycling of human souls. When the rains arrive – in particular torrential rains – it is an extreme release of energy and forces, and thus a manifestation of the god's power.[137] The rain, in combination with the rainbow, is a very powerful expression of the powers and wills of the gods, and some places in the landscape bear testimony to particular powers and excess.

At the beginning of time, ancestral beings travelled around the lands and created features on their own. At certain places they left parts of their spiritual essence, and the spirits living in such places (and in deep waters) are immensely powerful. Paintings whose colours 'leap out' at you and reflections that 'come out at you' transfer powers. Similarly, brightly coloured sunsets or bright reflections in water have positive valued qualities. Rainbows seen after the rain or rainbows reflected in water at important sites are seen as a 'reflection', 'profane spirit' or 'shadow' of the ancestral being.[138]

Cross-cultural patterns

The serpents know all mysteries: 'because of the ambivalence with which they are regarded serpents may be associated either with devils or gods … The serpent belongs not only to the water and the earth; it can also be associated with the heavens.'[139] Throughout the world, in many cultures and cosmologies, there are numerous cross-cultural patterns. These have already been touched upon, and only a few aspects will be elaborated further, since this is a research topic on its own; but a few references do have relevance for the Busoga case discussed later.

Lightning and the rainbow share one fundamental feature, which also includes perceptions of rain- and thunder-gods. Ever since the original creation or primeval separation, in many cosmologies they are the only surviving links that bind heaven and earth. Thus, according to Wrigley,

> Rainbow, in African thought, is a great snake which lives in water, but when it rears into the sky it holds apart the waters of earth and the waters of heaven, and must therefore be severed, beheaded, to release the rains. The complementary opposition of these divinities guarantees the proper alterations of the seasons and, beyond that, the inescapable rhythm of life and death.[140]

Among the indigenous hunter-gatherer groups of South Africa, the belief in Great Snakes with supernatural powers was a prominent part of their culture. Many of these snakes were closely related to the rain, and there were two overall categories: those living in and those living out of water. A Water Snake usually meant a River or a Fountain Snake, and the head of a Water Snake in rock-art resembles the head of a horse or hippopotamus. Moreover, not only is the Water Snake very powerful, but many refer to it as a doctor or a magician. The Water Snakes control rain and the water levels of a water source; and if the snake is killed, it used generally to be believed that the water source will dry up.[141]

The image of a rainbow snake or rainbow serpent is quite common cross-culturally. As an extension of this image, there is a widespread image of a water-drinking rainbow, which is a feature of mythology worldwide. The most common quality and characteristic of this rainbow is that it draws water up into the sky, whereupon it falls down to earth. Different forms of water can be drawn up, including water from rivers, lakes or wells. The rainbow may also represent danger, since it may grab both fish and humans alike when it draws up water. In Germany, there are stories that the rainbow drew up a shepherd with his whole flock of sheep, and in Livonia even a fisherman with his boat. In Estonia, it used to be a common belief that people were in danger of being sucked up by the rainbow if they were standing beneath the bow.[142] Also in Estonian folklore, the rainbow snake is the giver of rain. The serpent sucks up the water from rivers, seas and lakes, and thereafter the water is sprinkled back to earth as rain.[143]

Rainbows are always elusive and magical, and in particular the end of the rainbow has throughout history been invested with particular meaning. Once a New Englander saw that the rainbow's end was exactly on his neighbour's house; later he asked if the neighbour had found a pot of gold. The neighbour replied: 'If you had looked at it from my house, the end would have been somewhere else.'[144] Still, the rainbow's end has played an important role in the history of religions and civilizations. A common belief in European folklore is that a monstrous creature or reptile, like a dragon, is guarding hidden treasure at the rainbow's end.[145] Among the people of Kédang in Indonesia, there was also a strong belief in a pot of gold associated with rainbows, sources and snakes. Beneath the surface of the earth, great treasure was stored, and sometimes some of the gold came out of the ground. The most important springs were places believed to possess this quality of revealing a golden pot. Not only that, but the pot was originally in the possession and safekeeping of the ancestors of humanity. Thus, the treasures in the earth are a kind of spirit dwelling beneath, which may take the form of a snake.[146] The pot of gold is also a very common theme in the Scandinavian countries, which directs the attention to the wealth of the rainbows in religions and cosmologies, not in the form of gold, but rain and God's blessings.

"The image of a rainbow snake or rainbow serpent is quite common cross-culturally. As an extension of this image, there is a widespread image of a water-drinking rainbow, which is a feature of mythology worldwide. The most common quality and characteristic of this rainbow is that it draws water up into the sky, whereupon it falls down to earth"

Illustration: iStock

Since the rainbow is one of the few natural phenomena that exist in all cultures and all religions, it has also been a symbol for different religious beliefs throughout time and traditions.
Photo:Terje Oestigaard

Chapter 4

"Moreover, the rainbow may not only symbolize a
pact or covenant between God and humans, but it may
also represent unity and hope among fellow humans."

4. Rainbow cosmologies

'Throughout history, the rainbow is seen primarily as a symbol – whether of peace, covenant, or divine sanction – rather than as a part of nature. As a symbol, rather than a natural phenomenon, the rainbow can depart quite radically from nature.'[147]

Rainbows in the sky

As rainbows are everywhere, so are the mythologies that run through the world's cultures and cosmologies. This is intended just to offer a brief glimpse of the rich variety of rainbows in religion and daily life. Rainbows are visually presented in the *Epic of Gilgamesh*, which portrays a legendary Sumerian king who is supposed to have ruled sometime during the first half of the third millennium BC. While the rainbow is part of Mesopotamian cosmology, the absence in the ancient Egyptian religion is striking. There are a few vague references to cosmological bows and arcs that can be interpreted as rainbows; but otherwise it seems that the rainbow was of minor importance in the ancient Egyptian cosmology.[148] On the other hand, this is perhaps not strange since it hardly rains in Egypt and hence the rainbow would appear very rarely.

In Asian and Hindu cosmologies, there is a serpent in the upper world and in the underworld, which are connected by a serpent-rainbow boat – basically an arch of water connecting the upper and lower realms, with the earth in the middle. Since it connects the earthly and the divine realms, this rainbow may also convey the human spirit into the afterlife.[149] Apart from the python, the peacock also resembles the rainbow. That bird has a prominent role in Hinduism – and to a lesser extent in other religions, too. Its colourful plumage outshines even the rainbow, and apparently the peacock is fond of spreading its feathers when rainbows appear in the sky. In India, the 'peacock's dance heralds the advent of rains … In fact, the bird seems to have intuitive power to forecast rain, people say, for its call means "come rain".'[150]

In Western mythology, the Norse rainbow is the most legendary. The tricoloured rainbow bridge Bifrost connected the earth with the home of the gods, Åsgard. Giants and demons attacked Åsgard over Bifrost and the rainbow bridge was guarded by Heimdall. Described in the *Younger Edda*, the colours are not mentioned, but it is very strong. It can only be destroyed by the sons of Muspel – the giants of fire, as happened in 'Voluspå' (the first poem of the *Younger Edda*). There is, however, also a remark in the *Younger Edda* that Bifrost appears red, as if a fire burns on it, leading the way to Åsgard.[151]

In European and North American sailor folklore, knowledge of weather following the rainbow was built on actual meteorological experience. A common saying was: 'Rainbow in the morning, sailors take warning; rainbow at night, sailors' delight.' At sea, rain and bad weather tends to move from west to east; since a rainbow is seen in the opposite direction from the sun, a rainbow in the morning (in the west) most often implies that bad weather systems are approaching. If there is a late-afternoon rainbow (night should be understood metaphorically), then the rains are in the east and receding. Thus, since many rainstorms occurred in the afternoon, the rainbow was often (correctly) seen as a sign of good weather.[152]

Since rainbows are usually seen after rain and storms, they have also been ascribed the opposite quality of rain-stopping. Thus, rainbows have also been associated with death and even evil. In particular, malignant powers have been attributed to the rainbow's end. 'Odd as it may seem, the rainbow is viewed not only as a giver of life but also as a spreader of disease and injury.'[153] But if there is one religion where the promise of life eternal is connected to the rainbow, it is Christianity.

Christian rainbow cosmology

There is an inherent contradiction in the Biblical creation story: 'When the serpent deceived Eve and humans lost their immortality, the serpent eats of the tree of life and gains immortality.'[154] The serpent has, from time immemorial, had a prominent role in Christianity; but so has the rainbow. In Genesis (9:8–17) it is written:

> Then God spoke to Noah and to his sons with him, saying: 'And as for Me, behold, I establish My covenant with you and with your descendants after you, and with every living creature that is with you: the birds, the cattle, and every beast of the earth with you, of all that go out of the ark, every beast of the earth. Thus I establish My covenant with you: Never again shall all flesh be cut off by the waters of the flood; never again shall there be a flood to destroy the earth.' And God said: 'This is the sign of the covenant which I make between Me and you, and every living creature that is with you, for perpetual generations: I set My rainbow in the cloud, and it shall be for the sign of the covenant between Me and the earth. It shall be, when I bring a cloud over the earth, that the rainbow shall be seen in the cloud; and I will remember My covenant which is between Me and you and every living creature of all flesh; the waters shall never again become a flood to destroy all flesh. The rainbow shall be in the cloud, and I will look on it to remember the everlasting covenant between God and every living creature of all flesh that is on the earth.' And God said to Noah, 'This is the sign of the covenant which I have established between Me and all flesh that is on the earth.'

The Hebrew word for 'rainbow' – *qešet* – has a double meaning: it also means 'war bow'. This double connotation expresses a very direct symbolism for some rabbinic commentators. The rainbow was God's war bow; but it was turned upwards, so the arrows would be shot not towards, but away from the earth. Hence, it has been a common interpretation of those favouring the 'war bow thesis' that the rainbow is a symbol of peace, representing God's discarded war bow. God's undrawn war bow highlights reconciliation, victory and the defeat of enemies; but it also indicates that God is prepared to fight his enemies in a cosmic battle. On the other hand, critics have pointed out that in the original history, Yahweh has no role as warrior. Moreover, evil and the enemies subdued in the Flood were sinful humans, and the waters were God's way of fulfilling his cosmic task. Following the scriptures, after the Flood, humans were the allies of God, rather than enemies.[155]

The waterfalls of Tis Abay, just south of Lake Tana in Ethiopia, are spectacular. Particularly from October to January there is an abundance of clear water, which makes a wonderful rainbow. This rainbow is called *Yemariam mekenet*, or the Virgin Mary's scarf. It is seen as similar to the scarves that women wearing traditional folk costume tie around their hips, and it relates to the Biblical story after the Deluge. Noah feared the destiny of humanity and God's wrath, since he knew that humans would commit new sins. He told God that he and his fellow humans could not be free of sin, and he therefore feared that God would destroy them in a new deluge. God answered that he repented the previous act and undertook never again to extinguish humanity. As a sign of the promise and the new covenant with his children, a rainbow appeared in the name of Virgin Mary. Today, the colours of the Ethiopian flag also symbolize the rainbow and God's pact with the Ethiopians.[156]

Turner, in a different empirical context, suggests that the rainbow as a sign of the covenant should rather be understood in the watery cosmology of the original creation. The very History of Creation starts with water (Genesis 1:1–2): 'In the beginning God created the heavens and the earth. The earth was without form, and void; and darkness *was* on the face of the deep. And the Spirit of God was hovering over the face of the waters.' The next cosmological process was to separate the earthly and the divine waters and spheres by the 'firmament', which worked as a barrier (Genesis 1:6–10):

> Then God said, 'Let there be a firmament in the midst of the waters, and let it divide the waters from the waters.' Thus God made the firmament, and divided the waters which *were* under the firmament from the waters which *were* above the firmament; and it was so. And God called the firmament Heaven. So the evening and the morning were the second day. Then God said, 'Let the waters under the heavens be gathered together into one place, and let the dry *land* appear'; and it was so. And God called the dry *land* Earth, and the gathering together of the waters He called Seas. And God saw that it *was* good.

The firmament separated the 'waters above' and the 'waters below', and this solid dome-like structure was conceived as stretching over the earth, both supporting and restraining the heavenly ocean. The waters in the Deluge were regarded as coming from both the great deep and the windows of heaven. Moreover, the waters of the Flood were not just any kind of water: they were *hammabbûl* – and *mabbûl* were cosmic waters. Thus, the covenant promised that the 'heavenly ocean' should never again inundate the earth; in other words, the celestial waters above would remain separated from the earthly realms and water. From this perspective, the arched rainbow guarantees the covenant and the cosmological structure, whereby the firmament separates the water, as God said: 'the waters shall never again become a flood to destroy all flesh. The rainbow shall be in the cloud, and I will look on it to remember the everlasting covenant.'[157]

In Ezekiel (1:22) it seems that the colourful rainbow is explicitly linked to the firmament: 'The likeness of the firmament above the heads of the living creatures was like the colour of an awesome crystal, stretched out over their heads.' The rainbow is placed in the clouds; and set against the background of a dark horizon with clouds, it is a colourful and pregnant symbol. The rainbow is not merely a symbol for humans and the new covenant; for God it is an instrument and reminder controlling his anger and fulfilling his promise never again to flood and destroy the earth:[158] 'Unlike the prophet, the rainbow is a natural mechanism that God creates for Himself. Like the prophet, the rainbow also warns human beings; its appearance is a sign of God's (restrained) fury, caused by their corruption; both the rainbow and the prophet are needed by Heaven to stand in the breach.'[159]

Moreover, the rainbow may not only symbolize a pact or covenant between God and humans, but it may also represent unity and hope among fellow humans. In South Africa, after the fall of apartheid in 1994, the rainbow was the symbol of the nation's reconciliation and unity after decades of racial and political conflict. The 'rainbow nation' as a collective identification worked as South Africa's new civil religion. It was introduced by Archbishop Desmond Tutu, based on the biblical imagery of the rainbow as a symbol of unity and peace. In 1994, Tutu proclaimed: 'We are the rainbow people of God. We are free – all of us, black and white together!' and the rainbow celebrated 'unity in diversity'.[160]

Studies of rainbows and structuralism

Since the rainbow is one of the few natural phenomena that exist in all cultures and all religions, it has also been a symbol for different religious beliefs throughout time and traditions (Figure 9). As emphasized, 'religion draws its symbols not only from human personality but also from the material world … it is convinced that beyond the world of sense-data there is another world – a world of values'.[161] Also, and perhaps even more fitting for the rainbow, 'Symbol – the clothing which the spiritual borrows from the material plane – is a form of artistic expression.'[162] Symbols are therefore visualizations, where the visible stands for the invisible and the material for the immaterial. A symbol might be a material object, an animal, a human, a ritual or an institution; but a material symbol has no intrinsic value in itself; it is always charged with strong emotional meanings: ideas, beliefs and attitudes.[163] Moreover, as has been pointed out, 'Expression is the one fundamental sacrament. It is the outward and visible sign of an inward and spiritual grace.'[164] However, 'The content of a symbol can never be fully expressed rationally … We can make its rational component comprehensible to consciousness; its irrational component we can grasp only with our feelings.'[165] This has made the rainbow as a symbol very fruitful for structural analyses, not only because it is a natural phenomenon everywhere in the world, but also because of its place as a symbol, which can never be fully understood on the surface.

Without delving deep into the works of Claude Lévi-Strauss's structuralism (which would require much more space than is available here), suffice it to say that the rainbow has a prominent role in his theories, for instance in his *The Raw and the Cooked*:

> In South America the rainbow has a double meaning. On the one hand, as elsewhere, it announces the end of the rain; on the other hand, it is considered to be responsible for diseases and various natural disasters. In its first capacity the rainbow effects a disjunction between the sky and the earth which previously were joined through the medium of the rain. In the second capacity it replaces the normal beneficent conjunction by an abnormal, maleficent one – the one it brings about itself between sky and earth by taking the place of water.[166]

With regard to Africa and structuralism with a focus on rainbows, there is one book in particular that stands out. Luc de Heusch's *The Drunken King or the Origin of the State* has variously been described as 'a book that one will either like very much or else detest',[167] but also as 'representing perhaps the best example of the [structuralist] method practiced by anyone other than Lévi-Strauss' and as 'an African counterpart to Lévi-Strauss's mammoth series on mythologiques of South American Indian myth'.[168] The book discusses Bantu myths in a large area of Central Africa, including southern and eastern Congo, northeastern Angola and northern Zambia. Heusch analyses myths and epics from four major kingdoms: the Luba, Lunda, Kuba and Bemba.

Figure 9. The rainbow at Murchison Falls, Uganda. Photo: Terje Oestigaard.

Central to the mythologies and cosmologies of these kingdoms is the rainbow, and the title refers to the Luba King Nkongolo, who reigned in what is today the southern part of the Congo.[169] He was crude, autochthon and intoxicated, and he also committed incest with his sister. 'Nkongolo dialectically opposes Mbidi Kiluwe, the hunter demi-god bringing rain to earth and embodying fertility and the exalted qualities of divine kingship.'[170]

As Heusch asks 'Do the foundation myths of African kingdoms provide us with the keys to their histories? Or do they firmly lock the doors on such a prospect? Or again, are they likely to lead us on a wild-goose chase ending in the trackless wilderness of the heroic fable or the romantic novel?' His own answer:

> The ethnohistorians generally adopt the first position without feeling any need to justify their choice, and briskly ignore what appears to them as merely a mythological excrescence on the body of narrative history. In contrast, instead of brutally eliminating it, we are going to take the marvelous seriously: for we intend to reconstruct the mythological universe within which Bantu historical thought has developed.[171]

Given the focus on the rainbow in this book, only a few of the mythologies will be presented and discussed.

According to the myth, Nkongolo was the first divine king of the Luba. He bears the same name as the rainbow – Nkongolo. The rainbow made the celestial union between two serpents visible; one serpent was male and the other female, and they lived in two different rivers. Among the Luba, the rainbow was believed to prevent the rain and the rainbow serpent was 'binding' the rain and the upstream springs. When the two aquatic serpents join together in the sky, the fire they give burns the earth. Thus, this fire adversely affects the rain by withholding it and the rainbow 'burns' or drives away the rain. Nkongolo, as the divine king, journeys from one river to another (thus resembling the rainbow serpents uniting the bodies of water), but eventually he is captured and beheaded before being buried in a termite mound.[172] According to Heusch:

> The decapitation of the divine Nkongolo marks a separation of the dry (or burning) aspect of the rainbow (represented in popular belief as a celestial fire) from the humid aspect, associated with terrestrial waters. The rainbow effectively embodies a contradiction: at once male and female, it unites fire and water, high and low. Nkongolo's death connotes failure; he dies on a high place, midway between sky and earth ... The rainbow hero of the Luba epic fails in his attempts to unite terrestrial wasters (from whence he came) and the burning sky, of which he aspires to be the master.[173]

The rainbow has also been seen as the vapour – or the smoke – coming out of the mouth of the great red serpent named Kongolo. Nkongolo's decapitated head belongs to the sun and the dry season, whereas his body integrates into the aquatic natural order. Moreover, this decapitation of the rainbow separates the sky and earth, and hence fire and water, and this corresponds to the dialects of the seasons. Mbidi Kiluwe complained about the divine king Nkongolo's behaviour – among other things, he was not eating alone as prescribed, but with his fellow people. Mbidi's kingdom lies to the east, while that of Nkongolo is to the west; they are separated by the Lualaba River. The east is a mountainous region associated with the high and sky realms and the wet season; it is from there that the rains come. The western region, on the other hand, is low, representing the earth and the dry season.[174]

> At the cosmogonic level, Mbidi ... represent[s] ... the first rains ... The tragic death of Nkongolo takes on a spatio-temporal function; his decapitation not only separates sky and earth, it also establishes the cycle of the seasons ... The death of the master of drought is followed by partial resurrection. The preservation of Nkongolo's head puts drought in its proper place in time and space, denied the privilege of unlimited duration.[175]

In another myth, the role of the termite mound where Nkongolo was buried is elaborated further. Nkongolo as the python snake 'emerges from the termite mound at the beginning of the rains ... The termite mound has a pivotal significance in the Luba calendar ... it marks the appearance of winged termites and the first rains ... The fragile kingdom of Nkongolo is comparable to a vast termite mound, well protected against the rain, where men are engaged in gigantic construction projects.'[176]

Wells in particular – and water in general – contain seemingly a mystical and vital property, namely the principle of life.[177] Although the snake and metaphors associated with the rainbow are common in Africa, there are other cults that are widespread across the continent, like the Mami Wata cult. This cult, however, is seen as non-African, being primarily European or Indian in origin. Central aspects of this cult are snake charmers, exotic images and ideas; Mami Wata means basically 'Mother of Water'.[178] As Eliade says: 'Water animals, particularly fish (which also serve as erotic symbols) and sea monsters, become emblems of the sacred because they stand for absolute reality, concentrated in water.'[179] Pythons are one such water animal or sea monster.

Buganda water cosmology and python worship

Around Lake Victoria there is a belief in a type of Loch Ness sea-serpent monster. Indeed, according to Sir Clement, he himself saw one of these creatures in the late 1920s: 'A beast had come up from the waters of the lake and made an attempt to grab this man ... he clearly saw the head and the neck of the creature in the water ... Sir Clement well knew the appearance of [reptiles like crocodiles] and laid great stress on the fact that it had a comparatively small head, below which was a definite neck.'[180]

The Lake Victoria region is one of the core areas of python worship in Africa. 'The Bahima and Banyankole believe that their royal dead enter pythons, which enjoy immunity in a special reservation. At one time the kings of Uganda used to send messengers to ask the sacred python to grant children to the royal house.'[181] A person who met a python had to say: 'You are my father and my mother, be propitious to me.' Also, there were allegedly 2000 wives of the python god married secretly to the priests.[182] It has also been emphasized that 'Among the tribes in the extensive district of the [White] Nile sources … serpent-worship appears again more deeply-rooted and spread over a wider area than in the southern regions.'[183] Thus, Uganda and Lake Victoria has been a core area for python and serpent-worship.

The missionary John Roscoe published his *The Baganda: An Account of Their Native Customs and Beliefs* in 1911. This is to date the best documentation of the early religion and cosmology. In Uganda, according to Roscoe:

> The principal rivers were thought to have spirits, which were credited with powers for good or evil. Most of the rivers were thought to have originated from a human being. Thus, for example, the river Mayanja was said to have taken its rise from the spot where a princess gave birth to a child, and to have been caused by the birth-flood. The river was afterwards worshipped under the form of a leopard, which some people account for by saying that a leopard was drowned in it. The ghost of this leopard afterwards took possession of a man, who, when under its influence, gave his oracle in gruff tones and made noises like a leopard.[184]

Roscoe reports that by the turn of the twentieth century, python worship in Uganda was confined almost entirely to one clan and had a limited sphere of influence. The centre of this cult was an estate called Bulonge in Budu district, to the south, on the western shores of Lake Victoria. The temple was located on the banks of the river Mujuzi:

> The python god, Selwanga, had his temple in Budu, by the river Mujuzi, on the shore of the lake Victoria Nyanza … Inside the hut a place was prepared for the huge snake to lie; there was a log of wood, and a short distance from it stood a stool; over these a barkcloth was spread, so that the monster might lie with its head resting upon the stool. A round hole was cut through the side of the hut near the place where the log and the stool were placed, so that the python might go in and out at pleasure.[185]

The python somehow lived like a human, and it was probably trained to come into the hut, where it drank freely of milk and was given fowls and small goats. The python was believed to enhance fertility and give more children. Newly married women and child-less wives went to obtain the python's blessing and his assistance. Other favours could also be asked of the snake, but he was called the 'giver of children'. The main ceremony for worshipping the python was a seven-day feast at the new moon. The python was named Selwanga and Magobwe, which were names used for men. At certain times, the python's medium went to the Sese Island and requested cows from the god Mukasa to supply the python with milk. (The wife of Mukasa was a female python named Nalwanga, who was the sister of Selwanga; according to tradition, a brother-in-law has to give the occasional present to his wife's brother.)[186]

> The python was supposed to have the power over the river and its fish; consequently before a fishing expedition was undertaken, the priest would call upon the people for offerings for the god. On return of the expedition, the priest would gather the people together and make a feast; the people supplied the cooked plantains and beer, while the priest gave the fish. The python was regarded as the giver of children; young people living in the district invariably came to secure the blessing of the god upon their union, while sterile women would go long distances in order to obtain his blessing and aid.[187]

Pythons were closely related to the fertility cult and to women giving birth; but the whole cult and cosmology included the kingdom – and even the king. When the serpent-worship was elevated to this social and cosmic level, it shows the overall importance of rainmaking and the religious relations to rainbows and pythons.

> When a child was born, the parents were required to offer a goat and a pot of beer to Selwanga, or if they were very poor, a fowl was accepted in the place of a goat. Occasionally the priest went to the island of Sese to ask cows from the god Mukasa, because, according to tradition, Nalwanga, the python's sister, was the wife of Mukasa. The cows were not killed, but they were intended to supply the python with milk; they were brought over by canoe, each animal decorated with creepers round its neck. The King sent each year to obtain the python's blessing on his wives, so that they might have children … Once a year the god sent the King his blessing, and a present of fish caught in the river.[188]

Among the Busoga, there are some spirits referred to as *misambwa*, which also include Kintu. Ethnographers in the late nineteenth and early twentieth century working in the Great Lakes region showed how these spirits often manifested themselves in snakes, and commonly in pythons. Writes Neil Kodesh:

> Python centers … dotted the shores of lake Victoria in the distant past. These centers formed part of an intellectual network that elaborated upon the connections between pythons, the life-sustaining qualities of water, and the capacity of water to function as a mediatory substance [...] combining the connection between territorial misambwa spirits and pythons with spirit possession [and] fertility.[189]

This brings us to a more in-depth presentation and study of the water cosmology among the Busoga, with a focus on rainbows and pythons.

Photo: Terje Oestigaard

Chapter 5

"Each morning on a clear day, when the sun rises in the east, a beautiful rainbow appears over the Itanda Falls. The rainbow may be seen as the head of all spirits. It shows itself in the morning when the sun rises, but not when it sets. This rainbow is from – or is a visualization of – Mesoké, the mighty river spirit residing in the cascades. And Mesoké is the rain-god."

5. Busoga water cosmology, rainmaking and the rainbow

'The brilliant colors of many snakes, combined with their hibernation and reappearance after the first rains, might suggest a ready and spontaneous development of rainbow-snakes myths… The worship of pythons in Africa is fundamentally a fertility cult … On the whole, the idea of the snake visitor announcing a conception, is nearer to the ancestral-snake-visitor concept than it is to any other belief.'[190]

'Their supposedly sinister character and dangerousness cause fear; their enigmatic and ambivalent nature has led human beings to contradictory assessments of them: On the one hand, they are thought of as evil and as a cause of death; on the other, they are believed to embody beneficial and even divine powers.'[191]

The kingdom and cosmology of Busoga

The water cosmology has a prominent place in the traditional beliefs in the Busoga kingdom, and often there is a nexus of overlapping practices, where many believers see no contradiction between Christianity, Islam and the traditional religion (although the Pentecostals strongly oppose the healers). They go to church on Sunday, but they may

Figure 10. Itanda waterfalls. Photo: Terje Oestigaard.

also use the healers' traditional and herbal medicines when needed, and the medicines are believed to work only because they also involve the whole cosmological realm behind this visible reality. The causes of and solutions to malevolence and problems lie in the domains of ancestors, spirits and gods.

In all waterfalls dwell numerous gods, spirits and ancestors, and the divinities and spirits continue to exist in the waters even if the waterfalls are dammed (Figure 10). The Owen Falls Dam was inaugurated in 1954 and the Bujagali Dam in 2012. The Isimba Dam, located in the next waterfall after Itanda, opened in 2018. While plans also exist on paper for a dam at the Itanda (or Kalagala) Falls, despite the Indemnity Agreement, there are currently no political processes working toward the construction of a dam at this waterfall.[192]

It is important to stress that the water itself is not holy and the gods are not water gods (like Ganga in Hinduism). These are full-fledged gods like any other, but they prefer to reside in the waters, although they may travel wherever and whenever they want. While Christians may object to the term 'god' (since according to their beliefs there is only one God), in the traditional religion the terms (and understanding of) 'gods' and 'spirits' are used similarly and interchangeably. Moreover, sometimes there are different variants or aspects of the same divinity, but with various and particular powers; consequently the divinities can be understood in a number of ways – sometimes as a god and sometimes as a spirit with various specific qualities and powers. Both terms will be used here, since a spiritual or divine being with supernatural agency beyond this world is a god – or a spirit; in a cosmological perspective, it is not the nomenclature that matters, but their powers and how they intervene in this world – and importantly, which god is strongest and who intervenes most in this world for the betterment of humans, if the appropriate rituals and sacrifices are conducted.

The torrential and brutal force of a waterfall is testimony to the power of the gods; it is a physical and visual manifestation and materialization for humans to comprehend, but the waters themselves are not divine. They show the might and power of the gods, but the gods may also manifest themselves through other means – for instance, in a python – and they may intervene in whatever sphere and for whatever purpose. Some spirits are rather passive and not really engaged in the human sphere, whereas other gods are extremely active and interfere in most matters in this world. Itanda and Mesoké are among the most powerful.

It is estimated that there are around 3,000 healers among the Busoga; with a population of about 3 million, that means there is about one healer per 1,000 inhabitants. Since these healers also work as traditional doctors, the average number of clients that traditional doctors have is more or less the same as the number of patients that hospital-educated doctors have on their private lists. However, not everyone goes to a traditional healer, and some healers are much more powerful, with reputation even extending beyond the kingdom of Busoga.

The more powerful the waterfalls, the stronger the gods; and the most powerful gods have chosen one human representative as their medium and messenger. When the healers are possessed, the gods speak through their mediums, who convey their messages. Along the Nile from the source or outlet at Lake Victoria, the three most powerful gods are Bujagali, Kiyira (the source of the Nile) and Itanda. The healers chosen by the gods carry their names: Jaja Bujagali, Jaja Kiyira and Mary Itanda. In 2017, they were respectively 100, 44 and 47 years old. Since the water cosmology has been elaborated and discussed elsewhere,[193] I will focus primarily on the other mighty god living in the Itanda Falls: the rain-god Mesoké.

In Busoga cosmology,[194] there are innumerable spirits, including eight princely spirits. Three of the latter are Kintu, Lubaale and Budhagaali. These princely spirits have extraordinary supernatural powers and they may take many forms, including rivers, lakes or snakes. Kintu was the founding father and the first human being in Buganda and among the Busoga. Lubaale and Budhagaali are two of his children. It is believed that before coming to the Busoga, Kintu lived for some time in the east. Kintu is married to Nambi. One day on her way to Kintu's home, Nambi realized that she had forgotten millet for her chickens and turned back. She met her brother Walumbe, who is the spirit of death and also a water spirit. Walumbe started killing the children of Kintu and Nambi. Even though they did everything they could to stop him, Walumbe managed to escape. Since then, death has stayed with the Busoga and the only thing they can do is pray that Walumbe will not kill them.

The Busoga have been influenced by their Buganda neighbours, who refer to most spirits as Lubaale. There are different forms and perceptions of Lubaale. He is on the one hand a water spirit and the eldest son of Kintu. He is also seen as a soldier spirit made manifest in swarms of fierce bees or in the form of thunder and lightning; and also as a spirit of whom one may ask anything. Often Lubaale signifies God – the high God; at other times specific spirits. Each clan has its Lubaale spirit, to whom sacrifices are made – for instance after the first harvest of the season.[195] In practice, it is often difficult to tell whether people are referring to Lubaale as God and the source of life and the Creator, or to Lubaale as a clan spirit; and the concepts are used interchangeably.[196]

Nabamba Budhagaali is one of the real sons of Kintu. The name Nabamba stems from the verb *okubamba,* meaning to stretch an animal hide or goatskin. Nabamba belongs to the Waguma clan. The river Nabamba has a twin brother called Waibira, and both of them are called Kiyira. The name Budhagaali refers to the nickname he was given and stems from the verb *okwêdhaga* (to play). He was given this name because of his fondness for swimming.[197]

Waibira manifests himself in the form of a leopard, and it is said that he sits on a large rock in the forest. This place is icy cold, and such places belong to the Waibira spirit. The spirit is powerful, and a child can, without knowing, be taken by it. The spirit may disable the child so that it can neither talk nor walk. Sometimes this is because of wrongdoings in the community, and sometimes just because the spirit wants to show its power.[198] Importantly, some spirits are generally more difficult and hot-tempered; but there are many gods who can be furious and wrathful. And angry gods are not good for humans.

Mary Itanda and angry gods

'Itanda' means 'power', and hence the name signifies the characteristics of the spirit: it is very powerful and the forces in a waterfall are a manifestation of these powers. Mary is the only medium whom the Itanda god incarnates (or embodies through possession). However, at the Itanda Falls, Mary may communicate with all the gods and spirits, which also include Mesoké. There are numerous water gods and spirits living in the Itanda waterfalls; aside from Itanda, two of the most powerful are Mesoké and Walumbe. These are brothers and almost identical, although they can be distinguished by their tempers and wrathfulness. Mesoké is the rain-god and is always angry and dangerous, whereas Walumbe is more peaceable, despite the fact that he is the spirit of death. Bad luck is traditionally believed to be malevolence coming from Walumbe.[199] He is also believed to inhabit certain pythons (or else the python is his totem), and so killing a python is strictly forbidden. Killing a python will not only annoy the spirit of death, but as a direct consequence it may affect the perpetrator, and only a fool would lightly take on the god of death.[200]

Mary works as a traditional healer. Providing the necessary medicines is not a straightforward task. For instance, a good-luck medicine (believed to be potentially useful for any purpose) is based on ground-up grains from a special plant that is difficult to find. Even the leaves and the stalks of the plant can be used. However, in order to reap the full benefit of a medicine like this, it is preferable to have an all-inclusive package consisting of several interrelated medicines working together and complementing one another. One may start with a particular medicine to chase away bad spirits, which may (or could) be the spiritual reason for one's misfortunes. Then one may use good-luck medicines to fulfil the specific wish; and then conclude with coffee beans, which are for safety and protection against evil. Water is part of the medicines and practices, since 'water is commonly regarded and used as a liminal mediatory substance; it is shapeless, transparent, and dissolves other things in it, properties which render it suitable for a symbolic role as a transformer. Divination performed through transparent media is also common, and in Buganda found a typical expression in water-bowl divination.'[201]

Mary may also heal or treat physical injuries with herbs and massage, stressing that the patient should not seek medical treatment in a hospital, but should use her services. Given that there are so many healers in Busoga, the spirits are highly localized – although some gods are more powerful or omnipotent and work for the betterment of the whole kingdom. To some extent, the religion is based on the area or the village where the healer works and lives. Commoners in urban areas know little about this cosmology, unless they have a close connection to a healer.

Still, rumours and the reputations of specific healers may travel, and people from faraway places may come for a specific purpose. There are different categories of healers, both according to families or genealogies, and according to practices. Some healers work literally in the dark and perform their rituals and practices in the utmost secrecy. As an indicator, good healers work with an open door and bad healers with a closed one. If the door in the ritual is closed and the client sees nothing, but only hears talk, noises and shouting (how many attendants are present they cannot know), then the patient may suddenly be beaten by invisible hands in the dark. What other things happen in the dark, nobody can know or tell. Mary, on the other hand, works differently. Her door is always open and everyone can see what she does; she keeps no secrets from clients or commoners. When the divinities embody her and she becomes possessed, it is in the presence of the believers; and when she makes her medicines as a traditional herbalist, everyone can observe and follow what she does.

Apart from her main religious duty as a healer to please the spirits and protect their homes and waterfalls, Mary's other primary responsibility is to the people living next to the waterfalls. When the spirits are angry, people will inevitably die, and she is genuinely concerned about the people's welfare. The spirits need to be appreciated; if they are propitiated by, for instance, blood sacrifices, they may safeguard the devotees and show benevolence. But the gods' grace depends on humans' obedience and good behaviour, and on the appropriate rituals and sacrifices being conducted.

The destruction of the Bujagali and Isimba waterfalls has caused divine damage beyond repair, since the gods were largely excluded from both dam constructions. This also has an impact on Mary, her gods and the remaining pristine waterfalls. The damming of the Bujagali Falls infuriated the gods, and in 2017 – five years after the dam was inaugurated and about 20 years after the process was initiated – Jaja Bujagali said that the gods were still wrathful. Mary Itanda also pointed out that the gods living in the Itanda waterfalls are already very angry because of the dams upstream and downstream of these falls. Thus, even gods in a waterfall that is not dammed can be furious because of dams elsewhere, since all the divinities and spirits belong to the same water cosmology, and consequently one waterfall destroyed elsewhere may have religious impacts, at another waterfall.

Mary could tell that the gods at the Isimba Dam (located at the next waterfall downstream from the Itanda Falls) were furious. Even the World Bank has raised concerns about the Isimba reservoir. According to the 2007 Indemnity Agreement, as mentioned, the Itanda or Kalagala area should be protected as compensation for the destruction of the waterfalls at Bujagali (partly funded by the World Bank). Although the Isimba Dam was built by the Chinese, there are concerns about the filling of the reservoir, which may stretch as far as 28 km towards the Itanda waterfalls. The reservoir's tail end may thus flood parts of the surrounding settlements and even impact the Itanda (Kalagala) Falls themselves.[202] If this happens, the gods living in the Itanda waterfalls will be even angrier.

The Bujagali waterfalls upstream of Itanda and the Isimba waterfalls downstream are dammed, and the natural waterscape where the spirits live has been destroyed. Thus, these modernization projects impact the spirits living at the Itanda Falls, since it is the same water and river; and as part of the same overall cosmology, they are intimately connected. To use a human analogy for the cosmological world, the gods and spirits share the same genealogy and can be regarded as belonging to the same family (like Budhagaali being the father of Kiyira, etc.). According to Mary, the spirits residing in the previous Isimba waterfalls were extremely angry because of the dam, and general discontent in the spirit realm affects all, spirits and humans alike. Mary feared that she might suffer badly, since it is one of the main obligations of the healers to protect the spirits' territory in general, and the waterfalls in particular. If a dam is built at the Itanda (Kalagala) Falls, then Mary fears that the gods may kill her, as she will have been unable to protect the gods' domains – the waterfalls.

There were also other reasons why the gods were particularly angry. Usually, there is sufficient rain in Uganda, and the country is green with good harvests. However, in early 2017 even this region was suffering: the rains had been very erratic, unpredictable and inadequate over the previous 4–5 months. According to Mary, the rainbow was very angry and disappointed with people and the political processes. The flagrant failure by humans to obey the gods' directives and demands, plus the wanton neglect of the environment and the destruction of the waterfalls through the erection of dams, has called forth the spirits' wrath. One immediate consequence is that the rainbow and the rain-god are withholding the precious, life-giving rains because people are allowing the dams to destroy the beautiful nature they are supposed to appreciate and venerate.

Lastly, there is also the question of the new religions, and in particular the new churches like the Pentecostals. Apart from big dams, the gods' wrath is also because of the new religions. According to Mary Itanda, in the past the community would gather to celebrate important events together, such as the harvest. Society was united like a family, and the old religion was shared by all; but nowadays it is impossible to conduct such unifying rituals. Today, the new religions – and in particular the many Christian denominations – strongly oppose the traditional religion as pagan and heretical. The Christians say Mary and her followers have gone astray and are going against God's Commandments. The Pentecostals and Born-Again Christians are the most aggressive in attacking the traditional beliefs. Consequently, most people are now reluctant to conduct the blood sacrifices that the river-gods demand, and the former societal unity is also withering. The paltry sacrifices make the river-gods angry and upset not only with the former devotees (who used to conduct these rituals), but also (and more importantly) with Christianity in general and the Pentecostals in particular.

Between the gods in the respective religions, there is real enmity – or so it is perceived. On the one hand, there is God, Jesus and the Holy Spirit; on the other hand, there are the innumerable river-gods and spirits not only in the Itanda Falls, but all over the Busoga Kingdom. According to Mary, it is all about prominence – who dominates which realms and domains – at all time and everywhere. While some Catholics may perceive the traditional gods as fables or non-existent, many Pentecostals acknowledge their existence; not as different gods or spirits in another religion, but as incarnations of the Devil and his disciples. The battle is here and now, and the cosmic fight has consequences for ordinary humans. Not only do people go to hell if they choose the wrong path (according to the Christians), but it may even be dangerous for believers in the traditional religion, since the gods may kill people who do not adhere to the prescribed religious practices and (among other things) conduct the appropriate sacrifices. The water spirits may drown people in torrential cascades in the waterfalls; or, like Mesoké and the rainbow, may withhold the life-giving and desperately needed rain as a penalty. Angry gods

Figure 11. African rock python in the Nile Reptile Park, Jinja. Photo: Terje Oestigaard.

punish people and society, and one very efficient and powerful way is by withholding the precious rains.

The python, the rainbow and Mesoké

Each morning on a clear day, when the sun rises in the east, a beautiful rainbow appears over the Itanda Falls. The rainbow may be seen as the head of all spirits. It shows itself in the morning when the sun rises, but not when it sets. This rainbow is from – or is a visualization of – Mesoké, the mighty river spirit residing in the cascades. And Mesoké is the rain-god. Although there are many spirits in the Itanda waterfalls – with some stronger and superior to others (depending on perspective and which part of the cosmology is emphasized) – the rainbow is a physical visualization of Mesoké, and he is the head god of all the other spirits.

Among common people, not much is generally known about the python and its role in the cosmology. The python is a particular river and clan spirit called Walumbe (Figure 11). He may live in swampy areas, ponds and wells, but primarily in the main river itself. The great python is closely and intimately connected to Mesoké and the rainbow. The spirit Walumbe uses the python as a trail or vehicle when he moves around. Walumbe is also the god of death. The python can also be seen as another indicator of potential forthcoming rain, since the rainbow and the python are connected. If human genealogy is used to understand relationships between spirits in the cosmology, then Walumbe can be seen as a son or grandson of Mesoké, and thus there is a strong bond between the rainbow and the python. In other words, death is a son or grandson of the rain; this shows the close intimacy and dependency of rain, and the fatal consequences if it fails.

Importantly, although the python is closely related to, and is associated with, Mesoké, the rain-god is always invisible when he is on the roam: he moves around as invisible as a full-fledged god in any religion, and does not use a python as a divine vehicle. As a rain and thunder-god, he moves quickly over vast areas of the sky.

While a god like Itanda may choose to embody and become present in an animal disguise, like a lion or a python, Mesoké does not. Other gods or spirits, including Kiyira, may also use the python as a special embodiment or moving body. Some gods or spirits are apparently more bound to a specific place than others; they are highly localized to a specific shrine, tree or a particular body of water. Such spirits cannot move far away by themselves and may use the python if they are going to visit places further afield. The python is a cosmic mover on this worldly side, where spirits use it as a transport medium. Still, gods are gods and they choose whomever and whatever they want to embody when they move around. While pythons are the most common, other snakes may also be used, such as cobras or green mambas. Even birds are used by spirits when they move, if they so wish – specifically the rare and beautiful woodland kingfisher. It is small and difficult to spot, despite its very colourful feathers and piercing call.

When snakes are possessed or embodied by spirits, they are not dangerous. They are messengers: gods or spirits take the form of a snake to show their presence and to evoke awe and respect. The snakes may even bite humans; and even if the bite is not lethal, the attention and awareness of believers are heightened. Some people can always see the snake; others may not be able to, creating a special uncertainty about things. But snakes not embodied by spirits can be very dangerous, and people may kill the serpents out of fear; though the snakes are divine vehicles, the spirits and gods forgive people for their ignorance, since they are driven by fear and anxiety. On the other hand, if a healer kills a snake, that is a heinous crime. But then healers claim that snakes do not attack them, since they are messengers of the same gods that otherwise would embody them through possession.

Leaving aside the size of the python, snakes in general – and water snakes in particular – come and go silently and suddenly. They appear seemingly from nowhere, and nobody can know if they have just come or have been there for a long time observing people and their actions. If a believer sees a python and turns to draw the attention of others, the snake may well have disappeared by the time he turns back. This invisible coming and going creates uncertainty – was it there or was it just imagination? Snakes as divine vehicles are the perfect embodiments for gods. Not only may they enable divine beings to move over long distances in disguise, but their mere presence conveys what the spirits want: to send a message – the gods are watching you. They draw believers' attention to the particular spirit and to the fact that it has something important to tell you. A healer may later contact the spirit and convey the message – whatever it is and for whatever purpose. The python's main element is water, which also links to serpent-worship, rain and fertility. Seeing a python swimming in the river close to the source of the Nile is an extraordinary experience in itself; but knowing that the river-god Kiyira prefers the python as his divine vehicle creates a feeling of awe and mysticism. The gods are not only becoming visible, but also very much alive – and they are impressive.

The rainbow's principal duty is to procure rain. The rain-god sucks water from rivers and lakes, and through the rainbow the water is taken up into the sky, from where the rain-god may let it fall up his devotees, if he is pleased with their devotion and obedience. However, since people have been disrespecting the beauty and importance of nature as part of cosmos – disrespect that includes dam building – the rainbow refuses to drink enough water from the river and the waterfalls, so that the sky is insufficiently filled.

The gods work and dole out punishment according to their own divine rules. Obviously, it is not the common people who are building the dams – and in many cases they are against these modernization projects, since they are negatively affected themselves and often do not benefit from the electricity produced, because the cost is too high. Thus, it might seem unfair – from a human perspective – that they should be penalized by the gods for the government's dam building. From this perspective, they suffer twice: not only are they displaced by the dams and often reap little benefit from the economic developments, but they are also punished by the gods for allowing these processes to take place – even though there is little they could have done to stop them. Big dams present big challenges, and also create uncertainty about which means are appropriate and which sacrifices would suffice to please the gods in such difficult times. Thus, the dams create an uncertainty about whether the spirits will be satisfied with human rituals, given the massive upheavals in the natural water-world, when complete waterfalls and spiritual homes are destroyed. Moreover, who should instigate and be responsible for mitigating the divine wrath – the president and the head of state; commoners like you and me; or anybody and everybody?

Dams that destroy waterfalls not only disrespect the environment and the gods, but may also directly impact the gods themselves and their powers. Hence, from a divine perspective it is quite obvious that the impacts of dams are devastating; and the gods are furious. The lives of healers, rivers and spirits are intimately bound up with one another. As the river becomes more powerful, so the more Mary Itanda gains power and the more the spirit grows. There is a mutual and reciprocal relationship between the medium, the river and the spirit. The more force the river produces, the more power the healer and the river may attain – strength which they can later give back to the people and devotees. Moreover, healers accumulate power throughout their lifetime; and the older a healer gets, the more powerful he or she becomes. This intimate unity of power and cosmic flows of forces benefit each other and benefit through sacrifices. The more powerful the healer becomes, the more powerful the spirits become; this strength returns through the medium's body to the common people. The mutual dependency is kept in equilibrium, and the channels of increasing or decreasing flows of cosmos correspond to the actual flow and force of the water in a waterfall. Sacrifice, as a force for redistributing the powers of life, is key in this process.

In a distant history, it was believed that the spirits gave back powers in the form of twins, who were believed to be spirits or spirits incarnated. The destiny of the spirit or soul of a powerful healer is not like that of a commoner. Whereas common people may go to heaven or hell if they are Christians or Muslims, the spirit of a renowned healer might be transferred to another person, who then becomes a healer. The cosmic force embodied in a healer is a source of future power, and the accumulated spiritual capacity can be transferred along a chain of healers, ensuring the divine presence and access for forthcoming generations.

In the traditional religion, the soul or spirit of an ordinary person becomes an ancestor after death and takes up a presence in the divine spheres, among other spirits. The spirits of the deceased – for instance, dead grandparents – may approach gods like Mesoké and ask him to provide rain to the living family; thus they may draw the god's attention to the particular needs and deeds of the suffering people. Although the ancestors may have better access to gods like Mesoké, in the end it is up to the living devotees to conduct and behave correctly and fittingly. In practice, this means offering the necessary and prescribed sacrifices. Even if the gods' awareness is directed towards the needs of the commoners, it is the devotees' deeds that may ensure the life-giving rains.

Angry gods are a serious matter. But the gods are believed to be benevolent towards their devotees if the cosmological order is acknowledged, respected and maintained. If the gods are approached and offered sacrifices, they might be pleased and help the needy people. Hence, Mary said that if lavish sacrifices were made, there was a hope that the spirits may be propitiated. Nobody knew for certain, but sacrifices could give hope of some improvement in the situation of the local people residing in the area and around the waterfalls.

The gods feed on blood and accept all blood sacrifices, whether of cows, goats or smaller animals. In these waterfalls, the gods are not thirsty for human blood, though, and human sacrifices never take place. Humans should sacrifice, not be sacrificed. The more the healer develops and the more powerful the river becomes, so the mightier the gods become. Animal blood sacrifices to the waterfalls are not only tokens of personal wishes and appreciations of the gods, but are also part of the overall flows of increasing or decreasing powers and forces in cosmos. The waterfalls and the rituals conducted are true sources of power.

Still, despite the hardship and increasing struggle because of the drought that was affecting the harvests, very few came to the waterfalls to sacrifice to Mesoké. Although everyone needed the rains everywhere, the traditional rain-god had lost many of his believers. From a profane perspective, a goat costs a month's salary for under-paid hotel workers – a very high price to pay to sacrifice an animal to a rain-god, if one does not truly believe in the cosmological order and the potential life-giving outcome in the form of rain. The rain-god had been marginalized in the cosmology he defined.

Being seen as the head spirit, the rainbow deals with the most important thing: water. Apart from specific waterfalls like Itanda, where the rainbow rises each morning if it is a sunny day, rainbows come seemingly from nowhere and at any time. They are highly unpredictable, rare and generally never appear in the same place twice. When the rainbow comes to a body of water, it collects water and takes it into the sky, where the rain-god will transform it into rain and give it to his people. However, the rainbow and

Mesoké can also be very angry and decide to attack directly on land. When the rainbow appears on dry land, it is a sign that something is seriously wrong in the community – whether disobedience or devotees' failure to fulfil their ritual commitments. The rainbow sucks the already arid land dry of water and moisture and leaves it even more barren. A rainbow on land is a bad rainbow; a rainbow on water is a good rainbow.

Broadly speaking, Mesoké as a rain-god and the rainbow may come in three different ways. First, in a benevolent way, when he comes to water bodies and transports water to the sky from rivers, streams, lakes, swamps and waterfalls. Second, in an angry and malevolent way, when he may attack the dry land direct. Finally, he may visit specific healers, like Mary Itanda, whom he visits every morning. He may come as the rainbow; but he may also visit her by drinking water from the pots she has at her compounds and shrines. Having slaked his thirst, he returns pleased to his heavenly abode or continues on his way. A satisfied and pleased rain-god is good for the people and does no harm to his devotees.

While the Itanda Falls are the primary spiritual home of Mesoké, he also moves around to visit not only common people, but also other healers. When I interviewed Jaja Kiyira in March 2017 – the healer at the source of the White Nile – he told me that Mesoké had visited him the previous week. Jaja Kiyira and other healers also have special ritual pots filled with water in their compounds and shrines to offer the rain-god water. If Mesoké breaks the pot, it is a sign that the rain-god is angry. A broken pot is a clear message that something is seriously wrong. Although a healer like Mary Itanda may communicate directly with Mesoké, other healers may not be in the same ritual position. A broken water pot may nevertheless indicate that something is going on, since he is drinking from the pot. Jaja Kiyira, for instance, may not be able to talk directly with Mesoké, and Mesoké may choose not to convey his message explicitly even to this powerful healer, who embodies another of the most important and powerful gods in the Busoga cosmology.

Usually, when Mesoké shows his wrath, it is not because the healers have failed to fulfil their ritual obligations, but because some villagers have misbehaved and been sinful. Mesoké can be a violent and wrathful god, highly unpredictable, and can injure people. If Mesoké is dissatisfied and angry, he may bring illnesses and sufferings in as many different hues – seven in number – as the rainbow has. When people suffer from Mesoké's attacks, the body and sickness may take on different colours. When the patient seeks medical care in hospital, even clinical doctors equipped with the best and most modern technologies cannot find the cause, despite the most meticulous tests. Although the illnesses display physical symptoms – like the eyes changing colour – the causes are spiritual. While medical doctors will fail and the patients almost die from the pain caused by the spiritual attack, a healer can easily identify that this is the work of Mesoké. And the healers may also provide the necessary medicine to cure the patient.

When Mesoké or the rainbow first strikes at a person or family, most often the intention is not to kill immediately, but to send a strong message. If and when this happens, it is essential to seek the advice of a healer. The healer will mediate with Mesoké and clarify what is wrong and what needs to be done. Blood sacrifices are always deemed necessary, and one of the favoured places for such rituals is by the Itanda Falls, where Mary conducts and orchestrates sacrifices to Mesoké on behalf of devotees.

The healers also have the appropriate medicines and even preventive measures that people can use to protect themselves from Mesoké in case he were to attack in future. The rainbow's colour (as Mesoké) can be used as counter-medicine and protection: the healers may produce special pieces of cloth in the same colours, which villagers can put up inside their homes. If this rainbow cloth is put up on the wall, Mesoké will not strike and kill, for instance by sending violent rain or hail that destroys the fields and harvests. Otherwise, however, he may strike fatally. Use of this ritual cloth also shows the rain-god that the farmers respect him and his absolute forces: acknowledgement of and obedience to the divine powers is precisely one of the things the spirits demand of their followers.

The belief that Mesoké and the rainbow is a hugely powerful god is unquestioning among those who still believe in the traditional cosmology. Despite the ferocious, angry, unpredictable and violent nature of this rain-god, he is also seen as a benevolent and loving deity, who takes care of his followers. Since he is the master and guardian of water and the life-giving rains, his powers and forces are absolute. Although Mary Itanda is one of the few healers who have a special position in his divine and cosmological domain, Mesoké is not restricted to a single healer. He is seen as too dangerous and powerful to have only one: not only would his unpredictable wrath be a danger to that particular healer, but it would also be hazardous to all, since everyone at all times is dependent on his works and rains. If he chose only one healer, that would cause anger and mistrust among the healer's fellow men, who would perceive that they were not equally privileged in the cosmic distribution of what matters most to all: the life-giving rains in the right amount at the right time. Hence, there are particular healers who have the specific gift of being closest to Mesoké, and they can mediate with the god so that he gives rain – or indeed withholds it, if that is done in good faith (such as when the healers meet and there are great feasts for ritual specialists or commoners).

Life gives life – animal blood gives life-blood[203]

In March 2017, the life-giving rains had been highly erratic and the first harvest had started to fail; the precious rain was desperately needed in the right amount. However, as usual in the African countryside, when clouds do appear in the sky they may pass by village after village and not yield a single drop. But if one believes in the traditional cosmological order, the rain-god may help. In fact, this is exactly the time to approach the rain-god and to make the necessary prescribed sacrifices to ensure that the life-giving rains come. For subsistence farmers, individual and collective life depends on the rains.

In the ritual hut in her compound by the waterfalls, Mary called on Mesoké and announced the planned sacrifice. She smoked her pipe and shook her calabash; the smoke went up to the realm of the spirits and the sound alerted the spirit that his presence was requested. While smoking and shaking the calabash, Mary also started hyper-

Figure 12. The goat was sacrificed in front of the shrine and the sacred tree by the waterfalls. Photo: Terje Oestigaard.

ventilating. Wherever Mesoké was and whatever he was doing at the time, he reacted swiftly to his healer's request: within about a minute, he had come with violent force to possess Mary. In agony, Mary was seemingly beaten from within her own body, so that she trembled and shook and ended up almost half-unconscious. The spirit's physical presence lasted for only a short time; completely exhausted, Mary fell down next to her Spiritual Mother, who sat beside her during the possession. She is not Mary's biological mother, but her religious supervisor and mentor. The Spiritual Mother started massaging Mary's body, stretching her arms and fingers, while Mary shifted her position from lying on one side to lying on the other; finally her head and neck were treated.

When Mary recovered from the possession and regained her physical strength, on behalf of the spirit she welcomed everyone and said that Mesoké would be pleased to accept the offering.

When the goat arrived from a nearby village, all participants were led by Mary down to the river and the sacred place next to the waterfalls. Where the torrential force of the waterfalls was at its most powerful, a shrine made of bark-clothes and decorated with cowrie shells stood next to a sacred tree leaning over the water. All participants had to take off their shoes before entering the sacred place, and Mary, dressed in the traditional ritual bark-clothes with cowrie shells, prepared for the sacrifice. Anyone can sacrifice to the various specific spirits residing in the waterfalls, but it is always Mary who oversees, supervises and conducts the particular ritual and sacrifice as the medium on behalf of the devotees. She is the medium with direct contact to the spirits.

Figure 13. The shrine with the sacrificial blood. Photo: Terje Oestigaard.

The ritual started with some small sum of money being offered to the bark-clothed shrine. A few coffee beans were placed on top of small banknotes, delivered to the shrine with both hands. Thereafter the wishes for the sacrifices were given to Mesoké. Devotees always have deep personal motivations and reasons triggering the need for a sacrifice; these vary according to the individual's life situation and the depth of misery and hardship, but also according to the degree of religious obedience. Although the overall aim of the sacrifice is well known – in this case, rainfall – devotees may also wish for personal blessings, like happiness, wealth or a good life. These wishes are not uttered aloud in public, but silently, like prayers to the spirit.

The goat was then brought to the sacred place in front of the shrine. Again, Mary smoked her pipe, shook her calabash and called for Mesoké's presence. One assistant drank local beer, which was offered to the sacred tree and to another shrine. All participants knelt down and sat around the goat, one hand on the back of the sacrificial animal. While the animal was blessed, the Spiritual Mother drank local beer from a calabash, which she then spat onto all the participants and the goat.

The goat was laid out in front of the sacred tree and the shrines, and its throat cut by one of the assistants (Figure 12). Most of the blood flowed onto the ground; then the sacrificial animal was lifted up and the tree and the shrine next to it were sprinkled with blood (Figure 13). Thereafter, the goat – still with blood flowing from its throat – was carried a couple of metres to the torrential waterfalls, and its blood offered to the river (Figure 14).

After the blood had been given to the water, the dead animal was carried a few metres to be prepared. While the animal was being cut up, Mary, the principal sacrificer and the devotees were blessed with sacrificial blood from the ground in front of the tree. Blood was smeared on the forehead and on the inside of both hands.

The liver of the sacrificial animal was taken out of the carcass and cut up into small pieces (Figure 15). Mary and the main sacrificer were the first two to offer the river liver. Holding one small piece in either hand, they tossed the raw liver into the cascading torrents, while again wishes for the sacrifice were uttered in silence to the spirits. Thereafter, other devotees also offered liver to the waters. Afterwards, small pieces of liver were roasted on an open fire. The barbequed liver chunks were put on a small skewer, which was placed upright in the ground at the shrine among the roots of the sacred tree. The blood of the sacrificial animal was given to Mesoké; the raw liver to all the other spirits in the waterfalls; and in case some spirits did not like raw offerings, they got their liver roasted. All the spirits ought to be satisfied.

The ritual ended with a final sacrifice. There was another small shrine a few metres from the sacred tree, just outside the sacred area. Mary conducted the first offering, and thereafter everyone else followed suit. Four coffee beans were given, again accompanied by the expression of wishes. And then the sacrificial rite ended. The coffee beans were for safety and protection against evil.

When we left Mary, all the other ritual participants were preparing for a big feast along the river and the waterfalls. The goat was cooked on an open fire and the whole

Figure 14. The blood of the goat was given to the river and all the gods residing there. Photo: Terje Oestigaard.

Figure 15. The goat's liver was chopped up and given to the gods to taste. Photo: Terje Oestigaard.

animal was consumed that evening. It was a time of joy and festivities. When we left, dark clouds were visible on the horizon, though as far as we could see they brought no rain. That was about to change.

Mesoké manifests himself

I was back in Uganda in autumn 2017, and on Sunday, 1 October, I met Mary Itanda again. It was a joyous occasion – not only because we were meeting again, but more importantly because the good rains had come.

Mary could tell that the sacrifice of the goat had pleased the rain-god Mesoké very much; in fact, the rainy season had been better than expected. The good and life-giving rains had arrived and the harvest had been bountiful. Drought and a possible famine had been averted because Mesoké was highly satisfied with the sacrifice seven months earlier.

There had been other smaller and family sacrifices, where chicken and lesser offerings had been given to the water-world's gods; but only one goat had been sacrificed to induce Mesoké to grant the life-giving rains. There are no regular times or occasions when sacrifices are deemed necessary or compulsory: it depends on the devotees' needs and wishes, and some devotees are more obedient and faithful than others. Some may make a sacrifice every three months; others either more often or more rarely. However, the annual rainmaking ritual and sacrifice takes place only once a year, before the rainy season. Hence, it was a sacrifice for the whole season and the rainy period, and it was a ritual for the whole kingdom. As such, at a time when there could have been a drought, it was simply the most important ritual in the kingdom.

After we had been talking for a while in her ritual hut next to the waterfalls, we agreed to go down to the sacrificial place next to the tree, where the water pot for Mesoké is placed. Since we sacrificed seven months earlier and the sacrifice had been highly success-ful, there were no new sacrifices. A fire was lit and we sat down on a mat (Figure 16). Mary smoked her ritual pipe and the tobacco rose to the sky, announcing to Mesoké that his presence and attention were desired; one may request the god's presence, but he decides whether to make himself present.

Although I have had some experience of the gods and their presence from previous encounters, through witnessing possessions, nothing could have prepared me for the spectacular entrance of Mesoké. It was a sultry day with few clouds in the sky, but it was greyish, hot and humid. And while we sat – on the very spot where we had sacrificed to Mesoké – and talked about the god and the rainmaking ritual, it started to rain! This was not normal or regular rain, though: not many drops fell, and it lasted for only about a minute or two. The drops were huge and heavy, and they splashed down on us and on the ground – splash, splash, splash. The drops on the ground measured 3–4 centimetres in diameter! It was like a miracle and everybody was transfixed. We stared at each other, knowing full well who was making his presence felt. Even Mary Itanda was astonished: she had not expected such a magnificent manifestation of the rain-god himself. Following the cosmology, it was impossible not to interpret this as a

Figure 16. A fire was made in front of the shrine. Photo: Terje Oestigaard.

Figure 17. Mary Itanda in contemplation, with Mesoké's heavy water drops on her forehead. Photo: Terje Oestigaard.

satisfied rain-god, who was very pleased with the sacrifice that had been made (Figure 17). From a profane perspective, it was mere coincidence – or nature playing a trick; but from a religious worldview it is difficult to find any stronger proof of the reality and importance of a rain-god. The sacrifice had pleased the god, and he acknowledged our obedience and the ritual's success by releasing some big, heavenly drops of water that he had dragged up through the rainbow from the very waterfalls where we were sitting.

The gods' water-worlds and the water-worlds' gods

Even though it may seem a contradiction that a rain-god lives as a river-god in the cascading waterfalls, it makes perfect sense and completes the hydrological cycle. The immense and raw forces of the waterfalls testify to the extreme powers of the rain-god. More importantly, even rain-gods need to make rain: there is no rain in heaven by itself; the rain-god needs to procure it by bringing water into the sky. The waterfalls become the ultimate sources of the Nile, with the rainbow acting as the means whereby water is sucked up and transported into the sky. When the water in the river explodes in the violent cascades, everyone can see the water droplets rising to the sky. The water not only flows downstream, but also transcends to heaven. This is, however, not possible without the rainbow. Unless the water drops are transferred through the rainbow, they will fall back into the river and the waterfalls – as again everyone can see. And everyone knows that the rainbow only appears when there is water in the air, and from the sources in the waterfalls one may then see that water from the river is going the whole way up to the sky. The rain-god has created rain. He has filled the sky or heaven with water.

The rainmaking and rain-giving god Mesoké, the rainbow and the python form a complete hydrological cycle and logical cosmology. While rainmakers are often understood as ritual specialists mediating on behalf of people asking the gods for rain, this is only half the hydrological cycle. Rain-gods may give the precious life-giving rains; but before they can bestow this gift on their people, the rain itself needs to be made and kept in heaven.

The cosmology of Mesoké completes the hydrological cycle. The rain-god himself is in charge of creating and maintaining the whole cycle. Water does not appear in the sky by itself; it has to be made. Torrential rainfall in tropical areas is massive. One can only imagine the physical burden and divine job of dragging millions of tons of water up into the sky – only to release it and start all over again, day after day, year after year. From this perspective, it is no wonder the rain-god gets angry when devotees fail to appreciate the immense work – especially given that their lives and well-being are dependent on these rains. Surely the occasional blood sacrifice of an animal is not too much to ask for? And yet it seems it is. The consequences from a religious perspective is that Mesoké stops using the rainbow to fill the sky with water (or if he does continue, he does not give it to the needy – albeit ignorant – people who disobey and disrespect the hard-working and benevolent rain-god).

In a working and functioning cosmology, the role of Mesoké, the rainbow and the python – and their interrelations – are perfectly fitted to the local hydrology and cosmological order. The rain-god fulfils the hydrological cycle; he is the alpha and omega from where the rain starts in the sources of the waterfalls and to where it eventually returns after the precious rains have fallen on land and drained into the river. Water in general – and the waterfalls in particular – is the source of the rain that is made by means of the rainbow. It is a specific cosmology adapted and perfected to the local hydrological phenomena and environment; and it is a hydrological cosmology. Hence, water cosmologies and rainmaking rituals and tradition belong to both cultural and natural heritages, and to tangible and intangible heritages.

"Water does not appear in the sky by itself; it has to be made. Torrential rainfall in tropical areas is massive. One can only imagine the physical burden and divine job of dragging millions of tons of water up into the sky – only to release it and start all over again, day after day, year after year."

Thus, there is inherently accepted wisdom ascribed to these phenomena at different levels, and the very basic wisdom is that water is the source of all life; but like life itself, water also changes, challenges and contradicts life and flows of life. Water is the one and the many at the same time; it can be benevolent and malevolent; and the precarious lines and differences between the extreme existences of life and death are as fluid and as much in flux as life itself.
Photo:Terje Oestigaard

Chapter 6

"For subsistence farmers living in dry areas, the annual
rains in the right amount at the right time are a matter
of life and death. Great variability in the waters on which
all life depends tends to enable the development of religious
structures where humans and divinities interact and engage
in various ways of ensuring the precious waters – or,
in more general terms, wealth and health for all."

6. Rainmaking and understanding water in society and religion

'When the weather is everything – when it determines, in ways nothing else can, what will grow and how much, whether and how long people will do migrant labour, whether it will be a feast or famine year, whether some will live or die – it is unwise not to take such things very seriously … That the rain begins promptly and falls regularly each season – indeed, that it arrives and falls at all – is, quite literally, a matter of life or death. Without rain nothing grows. And without growth, people and animals will wither and die.'[204]

Agro-water variability

Although the quote above is not from Uganda, but Tanzania, it puts emphasis on the absolute importance of rain. Speaking from a water and food perspective, we have stressed the particular characteristics and challenges of African water and food systems:

> Although there are always hydrological fluctuations, this inter-annual variability and availability has been greater and more unpredictable in Africa, which historically has resulted in extremely robust resilience and risk-management strategies … The particular condition that has framed large parts of Africa is the great agro-ecological variability within even small territories: it may rain sufficiently in one village but not in the neighbouring one … If it is one thing that characterizes statistical averages concerning precipitation, it is that the actual rainfall in a given year is hardly ever the average: more often than not it is extreme one way or another. In other words, there is hardly ever a 'normal' year; the erratic and unpredictable rainfall patterns become 'the norm'. Moreover, the total inter-annual amount of precipitation is not always the most relevant measure. If there are two rainy seasons – the long and the short – what matters fundamentally for agriculturalists is that the right amount of water comes at the right time. In particular, rain-fed agriculture is highly vulnerable to erratic precipitation patterns. If the rains fail, or are abundant at the wrong time for the cultivation season, it may have devastating consequences.[205]

Figure 18. Light clouds not giving rain. Early in the morning at the source of the White Nile and the outlet of Lake Victoria. Photo: Terje Oestigaard.

Dams and irrigation are the most efficient ways of controlling this extreme agro-water variability and of ensuring (and securing) sufficient and predictable harvests year after year. However, irrigation opportunities are limited in Africa, and most people and farmers have lived – and still do – in the countryside that is solely dependent on the rains. Absence of the life-giving rains has been a challenge throughout history; but this is only one side of the coin with regard to extreme agro-water variability. Torrential rain, or too much rain at the wrong time, is as devastating as too little, and the whole harvest can be washed away within a few hours.

Today, in an era of water insecurity and uncertainty, the effects and consequences of climate change manifest themselves in the hydrological cycle with even more extreme variations: prolonged droughts and increased floods. In 2016, the World Economic Forum ranked water crises as the greatest global risk to economies, environments and societies over the next decade, posing an even greater threat than climate change.[206] Africa as a continent is especially prone to the irregular and higher frequency of droughts and floods; and even in earlier times – without human-made climate change – rain-stopping rituals were, in many cases, as important as rainmaking rituals. The rainmakers were often those who could also stop the malevolent rains; but if the good rain was withheld when it was desperately needed, this was often alleged to be the malevolent work of witchcraft.[207]

In traditional agricultural societies, it has therefore been of the utmost importance to control the rain; but this is no human matter – it lies in the divine realms. Gods and ancestors control the rain, and when rainmakers have sought to engage in the water-world and to control and manipulate nature, it has only been possible through rituals and sacrifices.[208] I will not seek to present detailed descriptions of the actual rainmaking rituals and practices other places, since these are everywhere different, and skilled ritual specialists have created a varied and distinct ritual dramaturgy.[209] Suffice it to say that throughout history the control of rain has been the domain of gods, and hence water, nature and successful harvests have always been part of religion and cosmology (Figure 18). With this as a short introduction, one may approach some of the premises of rainmaking practices and beliefs.

Understanding rainmaking

Although water is a scarce resource for the majority of people living in semi-arid regions, the importance of the type of water and the purposes to which it is put depend on a wide range of industrial, economic, energy, cultural and religious practices. Although physically it is the same water, holy water for rituals such as baptism, ablution or purification is in a different category from the Nile's annual inundation for irrigation, nomads' need for oases or water stored in dams for hydro-electrical purposes. This highlights the importance of addressing the way in which the different types of water are ascribed specific characteristics – and why. Water represents the one and the many at the same time, and the plurality of cultural institutionalizations and perceptions places emphasis on water's structuring principles and processes. Life-giving water is one category of water that has particular structuring qualities. It highlights the human population's vital need for a specific type of water at a particular time, whether for religious purposes, agriculture or daily survival. Thus, analyses of the importance of water in society have to incorporate the cultural and religious traditions through which humans act and reconstitute themselves and society. As Tvedt says:

> Systematic comparisons of the role of water in different religions has therefore a great untapped potential: (a) water is an absolutely essential resource in all societies, (b) most religions give water a central place in texts and rituals, (c) the paradoxical natures of water – it is a life-giver and life-taker, alluring and fearsome, creator and destroyer, terribly strong and very weak, always existing and always disappearing – mean that it easily can be, and often has been, ascribed all sorts of different and conflicting symbolic meanings of fundamental importance at a number of shifting levels [...][210]

What the crucial and life-giving waters are, why this is so and what type of water is available in a given society are all dependent on, but not limited to, different types of organizations of societies, modes of subsistence or agricultural practices (Figure 19). Nevertheless, the climate, topography and hydrological cycle – ecological variables which are beyond the control of humans in traditional agricultural societies, but which they nevertheless have to react to (today's dam building is one way) – create diverse water-worlds, where

Figure 19. Fishing boats on the shore of Lake Victoria. Photo: Terje Oestigaard.

both the amount and the type of water vary. Still, although beyond the control of humans, gods and divinities may procure these waters. Some regions and places receive most (or all) of their water from the River Nile; others receive most of their water from the great lakes or as rain, or from a combination of these sources, together with water from rivers; meanwhile oases and groundwater may be the only water source in desert regions. Hence, both the amount of water and how it is available each year – as falling rain, flowing river or lakes and oases – influence and affect the way in which water is incorporated into people's lives and worldviews. Consequently, the ways in which the various water-worlds or waterscapes are used practically, interpreted symbolically and assigned values according to local and regional traditions and norms are a result of humans' continuous and meticulous interplay and mediation of cultural and natural variables.

The absence and presence of different types of water sources and water bodies are of the utmost importance in understanding the cultural significance of water. The absence of water can be equally important as its presence – or at times even more important – in structuring a given society or region. However, not all water is the right water, and the problem is not restricted to its mere presence or absence. Too much water at the wrong time of year is as bad as too little water when it is really needed. In neither the social nor the natural world is water a single and uniform matter of life or phenomenon. The world of water often consists of a combination of various bodies of water, and the interrelatedness and seasonal variability of these different types of water constitute the waterscape in which people live. Thus, different waters are ascribed specific qualities, capacities and values according to both ecological variables and cultural traditions. People's ideas of water and the ways in which water are crucial for identities and values in a broader culture have to be seen in relation to which types of water are absent and present, or in which combinations they occur at a given time, because the different waters and constellations are actively incorporated into the collective body of knowledge, since water matters for humans at the personal, societal and religious level.[211]

From an economic point of view, an Indian finance minister once said that his whole national budget was dependent upon the annual rains.[212] Although this has changed partly due to industrialization and dam building, the importance of rain and rivers has not decreased – in fact, quite the contrary. On the one hand, the presence or total absence of water throughout the year is, of course, of immense importance when analysing water's structuring role in society. However, with an emphasis on the life-giving rains such situations are most often anomalies (apart from deserts, for instance), since absence is often followed by presence, and this puts the emphasis on the first waters. On the other hand, the occurrence of the first waters in the hydrological circle and annual cycle, whether as rain or inundation, normally attains a special and particular role in societies and in humans' perceptions of water, and this highlights which type of water is absent or present, and when. In those sub-regions where there is scarcity and/or great seasonal variability in the availability of water, such scarcity and limited or seasonal availability gives water extra socioeconomic importance and significant cultural and religious value. Most often the waters are included in the divine spheres or are assigned extra importance in culture and cosmology if, on the one hand, they include a dramatic shift from absence to presence (whether it is the first rains or the coming of the flood), and if, on the other hand, all life and death are dependent on these waters to varying degrees. Hence, in different sub-regions of the Nile Basin, various types of water are incorporated into society and religion; and the absence, presence and first occurrence of these water types are assigned particular and different meanings and structuring roles, which enable one to identify various waters in regional and ecological zones.

Belief in rainmaking and rain-gods is perhaps difficult for somebody living in a secular society to understand; but it is quite straightforward and logical, and by conceptualizing and contrasting different forms of rain, one may illuminate certain aspects. Having lived for sixteen years in Bergen, Norway, the rainiest city in the northern hemisphere (annual precipitation of 2,300–2,500 mm a year – even more than in most rain forests), I have become accustomed to rain – day after day, year after year. The weather gods gave Bergen a special Christmas gift in 2015: on Christmas Eve, the record was broken; by the new year, the new annual record stood at 3,101.7 mm of rain. In 2015, there were 283 days with precipitation – another record. However, even in a rainy place like Bergen, there are huge regional variations: only 25 kilometres (or 10 minutes by train) away, the natural topography meant that in the local community of Arna a meteorologist measured 4,000 mm precipitation. Although there are sunny days in Bergen, too, most often it rains for long periods: in 2007, it rained for 85 days non-stop (though that was an exception, although not a record). Obviously, there is no rainmaking cosmology in

Bergen (where anyway, in 2010, some 78 per cent of the population belonged to the Church of Norway – down from 85 per cent in 2006). Of these people, only 10 per cent attend church services at least once a month and less than 50 per cent regard themselves as Christians. More importantly, a rainmaking cosmology would make no sense in a city where it has always rained for 230–250 days in the year. And furthermore, there is no need for a rainmaking cosmology in a modern city where people are urban dwellers, not farmers. That said, no doubt during the damp summer months many would approve of some successful rain-stopping rituals!

From a functional approach to religion, one may thus identify at least two structuring parameters for the development and resilience of a rainmaking ideology. First, there has to be variability in precipitation (and cross-culturally it would seem that the greater the variability, the more likely it is that a rainmaking cosmology evolves). And that brings us to the second parameter: dependence on the rain. For subsistence farmers living in dry areas, the annual rains in the right amount at the right time are a matter of life and death. Great variability in the waters on which all life depends tends to enable the development of religious structures where humans and divinities interact and engage in various ways of ensuring the precious waters – or, in more general terms, wealth and health for all.

In Africa, these two premises have combined in many places, which can be analysed through agro-water variabilities. Although there are still relics of rain-prayers in Egypt, in the deserts (not the Delta or along the Nile) which receive scarcely a single drop of water and where there is no agriculture, it does not make sense to have a rainmaking ideology. Nor does it in Bergen, where shared experience suggests that it will rain, regardless of worship or sacrifice.

Figure 20. Why believe in rainmaking in today's modern world? Coca-Cola advertisement outside Kampala, Uganda. Photo: Terje Oestigaard.

In seeking to understand rainmaking, from a social and political view the role of the chief or the king is quite obvious. The leader is responsible for the wealth and health of his people. Apart from wars and protection, in pre-modern and agrarian societies, this was to a large degree dependent upon the precarious and life-giving rains in the right amount at the right time. This principle – that the ultimate responsibility of the state (as embodied in and symbolized by the head of state) is to safeguard the security and welfare of its people – is as valid now as ever, both in Africa and beyond. Leaders incapable of providing these basic elements lose legitimacy and risk being displaced, whether violently or not. In today's world, leaders no longer provide and secure the wealth and health of their people through rainmaking. Instead they seek to control the rain and rivers: the role of dams and large water infrastructure in agriculture and energy production becomes more important. That large water control projects may come at a high social cost is clearly shown by activists' opposition to displacement and often insufficient compensation. Former Prime Minister of India Jawaharlal Nehru celebrated big dams as the 'temples of modern India', and when he laid the foundation stone for the Hirakud Dam in Orissa in 1948, he said: 'If you have to suffer, you should do so in the interest of the country.'[213] Despite individual suffering, leaders are responsible for the health and wealth of the nations – and their people.

In the recent past – and further back in history – controlling the water-world and the rain was done ritually, whether the chief conducted the rituals himself or had ritual specialists at his office in charge of this duty. And failure to control the life-giving waters would similarly result in suffering. The stakes were the same then and now – albeit in different ways and with different consequences. Even past rainmaking rituals could involve the suffering of the few for the benefit of the many, since they could involve human sacrifices to please the divinities.[214] Moreover, given the seriousness of the stakes involved – all life and well-being for all – rainmaking cosmologies have throughout history witnessed extremely violent ritual expressions, with brutal and lethal consequences.

Still, a functional approach to religion and the development of rainmaking ideology falls short without the inclusion of the substance of religion – ancestors, spirits or gods – and the divine spheres in one way or another. Beyond the obvious functional and causal links – e.g. successful harvests in rainfed agriculture are dependent upon the right amount of water at the right time – a functional approach does not explain how the beliefs in a divine sphere cause or control the life-giving waters. In the globalized Africa of today, climate change provides in many places a stronger and more successful frame for understanding why the rain fails or falls; the ancestors may still exist (as may the Christian God or Allah), but they may not be primarily occupied with weather modification (although religiously they could – or perhaps even should – following the needs of their followers).

The rise and resilience of a religious cosmology structured around rain is easier to understand in past communities, where there were fewer competing frames of understanding (not only were Christianity and other world religions absent, but so was the global discourse on climate change) (Figure 20). But a somewhat more coherent relationship between water and food production in rainfed agriculture (or more generally, just life in all its various facets) can only represent half the picture – the functional aspects of a religion – because dependence on the life-giving rains does not itself produce the rain. In secular societies, too, life and well-being are dependent on rain and food.

In religious worldviews, the life-giving rains are created by gods or divinities. All divinities are invisible, but to various degrees they may also materialize and manifest themselves – through materialities; curing of bodily sickness, healing, natural phenomena – and the water-world. From this perspective, the central aspect – regardless of whether the gods are almighty (God, Allah) or have more limited or specific powers (ancestors, particular spirits working within defined spheres) – is the visualization of power. In religion, the major deities are by definition more powerful than humans, although there may also be inferior (and obnoxious) spirits or ghosts that, though not necessarily more powerful than humans, can still cause enough trouble to be a problem. The important thing is not their size or strength as such, but the belief that they exist and have various degrees of power that influence this world and humans for good or ill.

Changing water cosmologies and new religions

Water in ritual and religion is crucial for humans, gods and everything that matters in between and beyond. Cosmologies depend largely on water, both physically and metaphorically, to create understandable constructions of the relations between humans, gods and the otherworldly spheres. Since water is an element in nature and culture and is constantly changing its character while still being the same, it has transformative capacities that no other element has. This enables water to work and express metaphorical relations and images of contents that most often transcend consciousness; the contents are often beyond explicit comprehension, but are nevertheless real and implicitly understandable. Water has been used for purification in rituals throughout time and in many religions; humans have been sacrificed to ensure the life-giving waters; and water has had divine qualities or has been considered as entrances to realms beyond this world. The cultural and religious potential of using water as a means to construct the world has thus been almost unlimited.

The water in the hydrological circle includes rivers, rain, hail, lakes, floods, oases, swamps, bogs, wells, springs, rapids, waterfalls, snow, ice, glaciers, etc.; it also includes the transformation processes of evaporation, condensation and freezing, and each of these forms and processes can be perceived as either holy or sacred. The attribution of religious qualities includes ecology, because the absence and presence of life-giving waters are of the utmost importance in understanding the religious significance of water. The life-giving waters are for the benefit of society, and water is seen as the divinity's grace unto humanity, giving prosperity and life to humans. This water may not be holy or sacred as such, but the water enables life and human health and wealth, which is a truly divine aim and prerequisite for humans to fulfil their homage to the gods. In other words, these waters are essential prerequisites for humans to fulfil their cosmic purposes; and so even though the waters do not have any spiritual qualities in themselves (apart from being a gift from the divinities), they reveal the greatness of the gods. Hence, the seemingly neutral water is also incorporated into the religious realms, since humans are dependent on the divinities and cosmic premises for prosperity.

Water is absolute and monumental, but it can also be fluid and can evaporate like dew in the morning. Religious cosmologies incorporate all these aspects. Regarding monumentality and spatiality, the Marxist Henri Lefebvre had this to say about architecture: 'monumental space offered each member of a society an image of that membership, an image of his or her social visage. It thus constituted a collective mirror more faithful than any personal one … this social space … embraced … a generally accepted Power and a generally accepted Wisdom.'[215] Building and extending on this as a way of thinking, and bringing the fluidity of water into the picture, rivers, heavy rainfall and waterfalls are physical monuments in nature and culture, but are very different from static and built structures. Following Lefebvre again, the monumentality is eternal, because it transcends death and seems to have escaped time. Monumental space cannot be reduced to semiological categorization: 'I am not saying that the monument is not the outcome of a signifying practice, or of a particular way of proposing a meaning, but merely that it can be reduced neither to a language nor discourse … A spatial work (monument or architectural project) attains a complexity fundamentally different from the complexity of a text, whether prose or poetry … what we are concerned with here is not text but texture.'[216]

Although all human imagination and perception involve signification, where meaning is ascribed to processes and materiality, despite the fact that it is portrayed the other way around when divinities are involved instructing humans given the believed cosmological order, the shift from text to texture is useful for elaboration, in particular when analysing water as opposed to the static nature of monuments. On the one hand, although many monumental monuments are religious in nature – churches, temples, mosques, statues, etc. – and are also sometimes believed to embody the very divinities in one way or another, these are nevertheless built by humans. This human interference, impressive as it may be, by definition represents human devotion and entrepreneurship, not divine revelation as such or absolute holiness. On the other hand, the cascading thunders of Itanda Falls or intense lightning and rain, or annual and life-giving floods, antedate humans today and traditionally relate to processes and premises originating in mythological or cosmological eras and confirming the order of nature and between humans and gods: the divinities are superior. Not only is the water moving and powerful in itself, but it visualizes the powers of nature and the divinities, or more precisely, the powers of nature as created by the divinities.

Thus, there is inherently accepted wisdom ascribed to these phenomena at different levels, and the very basic wisdom is that water is the source of all life; but like life itself, water also changes, challenges and contradicts life and flows of life. Water is the one and the many at the same time; it can be benevolent and malevolent; and the precarious lines and differences between the extreme existences of life and death are as fluid and as much in flux as life itself. It is hence not only possible to understand and elaborate most of the changing existences of the sources of humans and life using water, but everything depends on these same fluctuations. This intimacy is traditionally never a human matter or concern alone: in religious worldviews, life – whose existence antedates and postdates this worldly sphere – originates in divine realms and is dependent upon it in all aspects.

By discussing water *in* religion and water *and* religion, we open up a Pandora's box; established social theories are thereby challenged. While the history of social science has generally regarded it as reductionism or natural determinism to include natural variables, such as water, in the explanatory frameworks, one may turn this argument upside down when it comes to water studies in general, and water and religion in particular. Spirits and gods (whether almighty or not) are obviously invisible and very powerful, seen from the perspective of the believers; and precisely because of their force, they may intervene in the natural world – and indeed, from a religious point of view they are the ultimate creators of all things. And humans do not live in imaginary postmodern worlds where everything is a social (or spiritual or mental) construction: the real world matters very much, and the right amount of water is a matter of life and death.

Believers include their water-worlds in religion, because it is fundamentally about humans and being human. Social theories that omit these facts are then those frames of explanations that on the one hand are reductionist in nature (since they neglect structuring parameters) and on the other hand do not include empirical facts presented as fundamental by believers. If the most structuring parameters are discarded because of ideology, by claiming that everything is culture, then these interpretations are deterministic, since they cannot account for lived human lives in a wide range of different ecologies and water-worlds. 'Data' means 'given' (Latin) – i.e. what is given to us and – in positivist language – what we see as empirical observations are independent and objective.[217] From a water perspective, with an emphasis on religion, water is analytically data; but more importantly and literally, it is also what is given to people by their gods or spirits, and fluctuations in the water-world create greater dependence on the divinities, since people's lives and well-being depend on this intimate relation.

Although there have been different approaches to including materiality and substance in cultural studies, they have been unable to properly address the complex and active role of water as divine agency and means in religion. Material culture study is a discipline concerned with all aspects of the relationship between the material and the social.[218] As Miller says, there 'is little point in attempting to distinguish systematically between a natural world and an artefactual one'; the main characteristic of materiality is its physicality, and 'to study material culture is to consider the implications of the materiality of form for the cultural process'.[219] Still, one reason that this approach has not been sufficiently capable of addressing water is precisely its focus on the material, with its specific etymological root. In Greek, 'material' (*hylē*) means in its ordinary form 'forest' or 'woodland'. In Latin, material or mater meant wood, but also mother.[220] Hence, both the reference to wood and what things are made of fits well in material culture studies, emphasizing artefacts and human modification of material and nature. It fits less well in water studies, where the physical matter is completely different because of its fluid and omnipresent nature, but also due to all the purposes it is used for without human modification; giving life to all species at all times but in very diverse, fluctuating and precarious ways. In order to gain a deeper understanding of the role of water as living heritage, one may compare two ethnographic descriptions of hunter-gatherers.

Living with water and each other

There are a few studies of hunter-gatherers and their adaptations and cosmologies in rainforests. Although slightly outside the Nile Basin, Raphael Tshimanga has provided some very interesting studies of the fine-tuned cosmological systems structured around water among indigenous people living in the rainforests around Kisangani in Congo.[221] Most of this area receives 1,600–2,000 mm annually, with October the wettest month (over 200 mm). Contrary to common perceptions, there are also dry seasons (relatively speaking) in the rainforest, which significantly structure the forest dwellers' adaptation and the seasonality patterns of the year. Hunting and fishing are mainly undertaken in the dry and early wet seasons. The late wet season is characterized by the collection of wild food, ripe forest fruits and honey, termites and mushrooms. Thus, although hunters, gatherers and fishermen are not rainwater consumers in the same way as agriculturalists, their lives and subsistence are very much dependent on the rainfall patterns.

Rain is generally known as *ngu ti Nzapa* (water of Nzapa), probably representing a heavenly genius whose name is often translated as God. Cosmologically, there are also differences among the tribes. The Wagenia is a riverine tribe famous for being the 'finest watermen' on the Congo River. They have developed skills to manipulate the flows in the cataracts and have highly efficient fishing techniques. Water is central to their initiation rituals, and their living environment is structured around the river, the bush and the village. The bush is considered dangerous; as one said: 'it is like a curse for us that we cannot grow crops; we are afraid of the forest as the forest people are afraid of the water'. They believe that fishing is the only subsistence activity that God provided for them. In the water live various aquatic genii; although not truly personified, they probably represent the very ancient ancestors. Because of its movement, water is life and hence a source of life, linked to fertile women who are bearers of life.

Among the Ngbandi, too, the spirits in the water are guardians ensuring security and provision. The forest is perceived as a region of wild beasts, and nobody walks alone in the forest for fear of the forest spirit – Kaina. On the other hand, the teeth of crocodiles are holy objects representing the force of the river, just as the ashes and the hides of leopards represent the secrets of the earth and the rainforest. The Ngbandi have strong beliefs associated with the intrinsic value of the different types of water: there are the spirits of the stream, Mbomba or Sangu, and the spirit of the waterfalls, Bekpwa. The latter spirit reveals himself from time to time as a rainbow, and the rainbow is both a snake and a dragon. The rainbow as a snake appearing before or after rainfall is seen to play a significant role in attenuating the effects of heavy and destructive rainfall. The real Great Spirit is called Kilima, and the presence of this spirit was believed to indicate that the river had taken somebody from the village who had drowned. Another malevolent spirit was Banda, who could poison the fish so that they became inedible.

Globally, tropical rainforests are the richest terrestrial ecosystems on the planet. Although they cover less than 10 per cent of the earth's surface, more than 50 per cent of all species live there.[222] The Upper Congo rainforest sustains millions of people with its very rich biodiversity; but also in such environments there are seasonal and regional differences that affect food security, water supply and the wealth and health of the peoples. And the variations and differences are invested with rich cosmologies. Even in rainforests (with presumably more than enough water), water in its many forms is a key environmental factor in livelihoods and relationships between humans and their divinities.

Colin Turnbull also had a fascination for hunter-gatherers, particularly in the Ituri Congo. His book *The Forest People* was widely read. In it he wrote that the forest is the father and mother of the people.[223] Hoping to find another group of such hunters and gatherers, he turned to Uganda. Although his next book was also a best-seller, he did not find what he looked for – he ended up cordially hating and despising the people he studied (as the whole book testifies). Turnbull published the book *The Mountain People* in 1972. It dealt with the Ik. Formerly hunters and gatherers, the Ugandan government banned the group from hunting in the Kidepo National Park, situated close to the (now South) Sudanese and Kenyan borders, and forced them to farm and collect whatever food they could find (although later studies indicated that they had been farmers for a long time). Turnbull did his fieldworks during times of drought, famine and misery, and he did the Ik the dubious honour of dubbing them the least human beings on earth; he only admired them for surviving in spite of themselves. He described a society in complete physical and moral decay: when people were dying, the others gleefully stole their food and possessions – no need to waste good resources! As he wrote: the 'Ik had faced a conscious choice between being humans and being parasites, and of course had chosen the latter.' Turnbull ended up recommending that the government should undertake a military operation to forcibly separate the Ik from each other, so they would never live in groups of more than ten – only then could they be saved from themselves.[224]

In a context of extreme hunger and famine, people thought only of themselves and how to survive. Even with a little rain, they hardly worked in the fields, basically because there was no point – their work would not provide enough food. This had social implications for goodness, which was not to help others, but to fill their own stomachs: 'a good man is one who has a full stomach. There is goodness in being, but none in doing, at least not in doing to others. So we should not be surprised when the mother throws her child out at three years old. She has breast-fed it, with some ill humor, and cared for it in some manner for three whole years, and now it must be ready to make its own way.'[225]

Still, in the past the Ik apparently had a functioning cosmology structured around water. The rain medicine was the most powerful, but in the 1960s that was the medicine they believed in least. It was also held by neighbouring groups that the Ik were the only true rainmakers in an era now gone. Rain dances were part of the rainmaking ceremonies, and in almost every village there was a rain-tree. Gifts of beer, meat and pots of seeds were placed around the tree, and the horns of a sacrificed goat were placed in it. When Turnbull did his fieldworks in the 1960s, however, the Ik claimed that they had no power to make rain, or even knowledge of how to do so. 'The rainbow for them meant that the rain was stopped, perhaps by a curse, when it should have continued, and that particular rain would never come back. That is all, or almost all: their name for God is Didiwari, and didi means rain.'[226]

If they once were great rainmakers, now the rain just meant more frustrations because of its unpredictability; it made life bitterer by its destructiveness. After two years of drought and famine, Turnbull came back to see the harvest for the first time in three years, after the good rains had eventually appeared. The fields were at first sight promising; but a closer look revealed that they were rotting due to sheer neglect; destroyed by baboons and eaten by birds and insects. The Ik said there were too few of them to guard the fields; but even when there were people available, they did not bother. There was so much food that they could not eat it in any case, so why not let the birds and baboons get a share? But even when all had their fields full, they were still stealing from each other. The Ik had full bellies and it was a good year. What the next year would bring was another matter and something to think and worry about then. Even tomorrow was not a concern.[227]

Turnbull's book about the Ik was virtually the only one about this people when it was published. Not surprisingly, it was heavily criticized and has been seen as one of the most controversial anthropological books ever. Not only were there numerous factual errors, but later studies showed that the state of affairs was not as bad as Turnbull had described. Many of Turnbull's informants dismissed the way they were portrayed.[228] Fredrik Barth bitterly condemned the book in 1974: the book was symptomatic of the crisis in anthropology, and it should be sanctioned and held up as a warning to all anthropologists. 'It is emotionally either dishonest or superficial. It is deeply misleading to the public it sets out to inform. Most disturbingly, it is grossly irresponsible and harmful to its unwitting objects of study,' wrote Barth. He highlighted Turnbull's own attitude, which 'ultimately must have developed into a paranoid hate towards the people he lived among so all genuine anthropological ballast is lost'.[229] The debate about the book continued in the following decades. It would have been impossible to publish it in later years – on ethical and epistemological grounds. And even the Ik investigated the possibility of taking Turnbull to court. Still, some later reviewers were more positive, emphasizing not the Ik ethnography, but what it can say to us about our humanity in the West.[230] In this sense, it mirrors much of the writing about Africa: it is not about the lives of Africans, but about how it shapes others' lives.[231]

Aside from all the criticism of Turnbull, these case studies point to the role and importance of a water ideology and the potential severe consequences if the ideology does not fit the actual social systems or ways of life. In many places in the Congo rainforest a finely tuned cosmology has been integrated into the ecology – or the other way around, depending on whether or not one takes a religious perspective. Regardless of Turnbull's disdain for the Ik, what he showed was how the absence of rain impacts all aspects of society; it was a water cosmology, but a water religion that did not function and was not adapted to the ecology and ways of life in all their social complexity. Thus, the role of living traditions as heritage and a rich resource for the future cannot be stressed enough; and the barrenness of dry fields thirsting for rain is an ultimate source of poverty. Plenty or poverty is a matter of the right amount of rain at the right time. Thus, not only a heritage, but the living traditions structured around water and rain-making have been the very sources of lives – both literally and metaphorically.

This adds another level of complexity. Water is tangible and intangible at the same time, and the physical forms constantly change quality and character, arrive and disappear – absences are as common as presences. Water evaporates; it falls as rain with varying degrees of intensity and coolness on fields and into rivers and lakes; it can be stagnant or else flow ferociously; one may collect it in pots or buckets; drink it and use it for cooking and washing; and much more. Very concretely, when drunk it gives life; and each and every human has to drink it daily to survive. In all aspects of life, it is the fundamental essence – from the grass that animals feed on to the fields that humans cultivate and harvest. And the food is prepared with the ingredients being cooked in more water to make a meal. Hence, water is commonly used metaphorically in narratives explaining such traditions, and in the creation of heritages and continuities of legends.

In the history of the Nile throughout the ages, there has always been great and vivid elaborations of this mighty river, putting emphasis on the need to include natural variables in the social explanations and water's role in culture and civilization, and constitutions of religions. Hence, 'in a long-term historical and ecological perspective, the Nile should most fruitfully be seen as an a priori existing, supra-individual and changing order which in various ways and to different degrees has framed human action and development efforts', writes Terje Tvedt.[232]

Water-society systems

Acknowledgement of the role of nature – or more specifically water – has largely been neglected, and most social researchers have been reluctant either to accept that natural constraints impact human behaviour or to credit the possibilities that certain natural elements create. This relates to the long tradition and discussion regarding methodological collectivism and individualism as two ideal types of historical explanation: the former is holistic and the latter is individualistic, where 'An idealist is one who denies ontological reality to matter; a materialist to mind.'[233] Among others, Bruno Latour has aimed to overcome this duality by introducing hybridity and concepts like 'actor-network';[234] but to a large extent it has either socialized nature or simply dissolved the whole dichotomy:

> Nature and Society have no more existence than West and East. They become convenient and relative reference points that moderns use to differentiate inter-

mediaries, some of which are called 'natural' and others 'social', while still others are termed 'purely natural' and others 'purely social', and yet others are considered 'not only' natural 'but also' a little bit social.[235]

However, water is both social and natural at the same time. The water stored in the ice in Antarctica has never been touched by humans – until now, when human-induced climate change has caused the ice to melt. Thus, water has existed – and still does exist – independently of humans as an element of nature; but at the same time the hydrological cycle has united nature and society from time immemorial, because of all the water-society confluences and dependencies, which also include religion and the life-giving rains. Even holy water from springs forms part of the hydrological cycle, emphasizing how and why certain types of water become holy and part of the divine world, while at the same time being part of nature.

From other perspectives, both Pierre Bourdieu and Anthony Giddens have aimed to solve the problem of combining structure and agency, although both sociologists have been working within the paradigm of explaining social facts by means of other social facts.[236] As is seen with the Busoga water cosmology, analysing religion as solely social facts is problematic (although people's experience of religion is also inevitably a social or cultural process). Moreover, this sociological approach is problematic because it aims to dissolve and erase both tradition and nature. As Giddens argues:

> For hundreds of years, people worried about what nature could do to us – earthquakes, floods, plagues, bad harvests and so on. At a certain point, somewhere over the past fifty years or so, we stopped worrying so much about what nature could do to us, and we started worrying more about what we have done to nature … It is a society which lives 'after nature'.[237]

Claiming that societies are living 'after nature' is a highly Eurocentric, urban and 'modern' approach that dismisses the main consequences of climate change and alteration in the hydrological cycle. Moreover, for subsistence farmers standing in barren fields, waiting for the erratic rains that have failed again, it is not life 'after nature' – it is poverty and suffering caused by nature. Following Tvedt again:

> The atmosphere traps the moisture of the earth, so the amount of water on the planet is more or less constant, and the water we drink is the water that the dinosaurs drank. There is no such thing as 'new' water, and it is impossible to describe water as undergoing a 'birth, youth, mature period and death', a much-used metaphor for historical periodization and for life itself. But since the water that falls as rain today is the same water that fell on prehistoric man, the dinosaurs and the earliest forms of life on earth, nature is engaged in a never-ending process of recycling our planet's water. Rainfall lands on the earth, heat evaporates the water, the vapour rises and cools and forms clouds, and once again the rain falls. Water's time is therefore both cyclical and eternal. There is no new water to create,

> and there is no old water to lose, and therefore the relationships of societies with this resource are very different from their relationships with other controllable resources.[238]

Hence, the role of water in history and society must be included; and it can be analysed from a water-society perspective. All water systems can be understood as consisting of three interconnected layers. The first addresses the physical form and behaviour of actual waterscapes at any given place. This includes precipitation, evaporation, how rivers run within the landscape and how much water they contain throughout the year and seasons, and the relationship between rivers and the sea, and so on. The second analytical layer addresses human modifications and adaptations to the actual water-worlds and the innumerable ways in which people in different societies have utilized water (Figure 21). This is not nature reduction, but rather the contrary, since certain waterscapes create huge social opportunities for welfare and betterment, but the very same waterscapes are, for instance, severely impacted by agro-water variabilities, which create obstacles and hardships. The third and final analytical layer addresses cultural concepts and ideas of water and water systems, including management practices and religious belief, since all practices are socially and culturally situated and constituted. These layers should be seen as analytical and not hierarchical or indicating a priority of relevance.[239] In an analysis, one may focus on one or all layers; or – as in this study – on where the rainfed agricultural systems are the setting and context for understanding the rich rainmaking cosmology, which belongs to level three.

Figure 21. Fishermen on the lake. Photo: Terje Oestigaard.

From a hydrological and historical point of view, the hydrological cycle and the water-world exist independently of humans; but humans do not live independently of the water-world (and today the relationship is intimate because of climate change). Since the water-worlds are all-encompassing frames of experience and living, in many cases they parallel cosmologies, which are also total frames of experience, explanations and channels of interactions with the divinities. Hence, understanding the role of water in history and society is an invaluable source of heritage, combining both tangible and intangible heritage, and cultural and natural heritage. Since water is the ultimate source of life, it has always been valued and will continue to be at the core of cultural, societal and religious developments.

John Hanning Speke arrived at the outlet of Lake Victoria, on the border between the Buganda and Busoga kingdoms, on 28 July 1862. He identified and defined this as the source of the White Nile. Speke was the first to document these societies, and hence his books are the first written accounts of the ethnography in this region.   Photo:Terje Oestigaard

Chapter 7

"It may seem absurd today to question whether Africa
has history and whether Africans are (and always have
been) active historical actors; but the denial or downplaying
of these two fundamental premises long dominated
discourses on African history."

7. History and heritage

'The Nile, as both the site of the early beginnings as well as the space of mysterious diversity, has captured the human imagination since the earliest civilizations have resided along its banks. The enigma of its sources, the life it gave to barren areas, and the capricious nature of its vital flow have produced endless speculations and legends. The realities and myths of the river personified have been retold and reproduced from the early ancient times to the present.'[240]

Uneven histories – and futures

Before returning to Mary Itanda and the rich cultural heritage of the Busoga – including rainbows and rainmaking – it would be useful to contextualize history and heritage in Africa, and to present a short account of this history. Although quite well known, it is worth recalling parts of this history, since the consequence and implications are still structuring not only historical disciplines, but also societal developments – and not the least the role of heritage for the future. If history and heritage are important – or the past in the broad sense is important, including living traditions – then it is necessary to emphasize this, since uneven histories create uneven futures.

A dark research history of the alleged 'black and dark continent' without history

'Africa's place as a prime contributor to the history of human development and civilization is generally accepted today. Across the ages, the continent played host to diverse cultures and striking civilizations', says Oyebade.[241] Thus, it may seem absurd today to question whether Africa has history and whether Africans are (and always have been) active historical actors; but the denial or downplaying of these two fundamental premises long dominated discourses on African history. The concepts of 'history' and 'agency' have therefore been intrinsically linked with the consequences in order to understand Africans within and beyond the continent and their role in global history: Africa has been portrayed as a black continent without history or agency.

The debate on colonial history and its actors has been referred to and discussed in length. Kipling described the Africans as 'half-devil and half-child',[242] although he is better remembered for his oft-quoted phrase from 1899 'the white man's burden', expressing the European colonial attitude at that time towards the perceived state of development in Africa and the responsibility of Christians. Africa was primitive and backward, and a continent without history or agency. At the same time, the German philosopher Hegel stated that Africa 'is no historical part of the World; it has no movement or development to exhibit. Historical movements in it – that is in its northern part – belong to the Asiatic or European World.'[243] Africans were not only perceived as barbaric and, in evolutionary terms, backward; but Africans were 'capable of no development or culture, and as we see them at this day, such have they always been'.[244] This notion of Africa as the dark continent and somehow backward linger on to various degrees; this was evident, for instance, in a speech made by former French President Sarkozy in Dakar in 2007, when, among other things, he stated that '[t]he tragedy of Africa is that the African has not fully entered into history ... They have never really launched themselves into the future.' This remark was said by Achille Mbembe to reflect an attitude 'worthy of the 19th century'.[245]

Although such perceptions may still exist in the broader cultural sphere, this is no longer the dominant academic position. The task of writing African history may also be seen in relation to the actual knowledge available, but also what knowledge has been available on which premises. In order to get a glimpse of the discourse hegemony of African studies in the 1960s, one may look at two processes that happened in parallel at the universities of Cambridge and Oxford. In the late 1950s in Cambridge, the syndics of the Cambridge University Press started exploring the possibility of embarking on a Cambridge History of Africa, but were advised that it would be preferable to wait, since hardly any serious appraisal of the African past had been made prior to 1948, when studies of Africa south of the Sahara started to emerge and when universities outside Africa started placing some emphasis on African history. Still, it was realized that there was an urgent need for such a forum, and so in 1960, Cambridge University Press launched *The Journal of African History*. In 1966, the editors of this journal accepted the mission to become the editors of the *Cambridge History of Africa*, published in eight volumes between 1975 and 1986.[246]

In the *Cambridge History of Africa* (1978) it was pointed out:

> In some respects, too, southern European people, most notably the Greeks and the Romans, appear as more active and positive proponents of the common civilization than do African people. But perhaps this is less a matter of history than of the perspective that is current today [...] in a European cultural tradition which can be traced back to ancient Greece and Rome. Such historians have not unnaturally tended to stress the European development of the original inheritance from the Near East, and they have given relatively little attention to what was achieved by Africans on the basis of the same inheritance, which they have received often more directly. It is therefore easy to overlook how much of common world civilization during the period covered in this volume was in fact developed in Africa.[247]

The diffusionist paradigm from the Near East is clearly visible. Nevertheless, with this as the intellectual background and point of departure, the developments in Africa were emphasized: 'it may certainly be claimed that the independent development by sub-Saharan Africans of their own foundations for civilization, followed by their rapid distribution of these foundations throughout the world's largest tropical land mass, an environment particularly hostile to the growth of civilization, should rank among the major achievements of human history'.[248] However, as has been pointed out, even the *Cambridge History of Africa,* in particular the last volumes, have a Eurocentric bias.[249] Still, this is rather minor compared to the impact of the biased works and ideas of the distinguished Oxford professor Hugh Trevor-Roper. In the words of Trevor-Roper:

> Undergraduates, seduced, as always, by the changing breath of journalistic fashion, demand that they should be taught the history of black Africa. Perhaps, in the future, there will be some African history to teach. But at present, there is none, or very little: there is only the history of the Europeans in Africa. The rest is largely darkness, like the history of pre-European, pre-Columbian America. And darkness is not a subject for history.[250]

Much could be said about this, but in some cases it is better to let the author speak for himself. Trevor-Roper continues:

> I do not deny that men existed even in dark countries in dark centuries, nor that they had political life and culture, interesting to sociologists and anthropologists; but history, I believe, is essentially a form of movement, and purposive movement too. It is not a mere phantasmagoria of changing shapes and costumes, of battles and conquests, dynasties and usurpations, social forms and social disintegration. If all history is equal, as some now believe, there is no reason why we should study one section of it rather than another; for certainly we cannot study it all. Then indeed we may neglect our own history and amuse ourselves with unrewarding gyrations of barbarous tribes in picturesque but irrelevant corners of the globe: tribes whose chief function in history, in my opinion, is to show to the present an image of the past from which, by history, it has escaped.[251]

Trevor-Roper thus defines history and the purpose of history: 'history, or rather the study of history, has a purpose. We study it not merely for amusement – though it can be amusing – but in order to discover how we have come to where we are.'[252] The European bias is explicit and, according to Trevor-Roper, there is no reason to be ashamed of that:

> It may well be that the future will be the future of non-European peoples: that the 'colonial' peoples of Africa and Asia will inherit that primacy in the world which the 'imperialist' West can no longer sustain … But even if that should happen, it would not alter the past. The new rulers of the world, whoever they may be, will inherit a position that has been built up by Europe, and by Europe alone. It is European techniques, European examples, European ideas which have shaken the non-European world out of its past – out of barbarism in Africa, out of the far older, slower, more majestic civilization in Asia; and the history of the world, for the last five centuries, in so far as it has significance, has been European history. I do not think we need to make any apology if our study of history is Europa-centric.[253]

In the due course of the colonial history of Africa, it is perhaps not surprising that also this has been stated. What is more surprising, is that it was proclaimed by a distinguished Oxford professor, and that it was said in the 1960s and repeated on several occasions. In 1963, Trevor-Roper gave a series of lectures at Sussex University, which were broadcast by BBC television. These were then published in a popular book entitled *The Rise of Christian Europe* in 1965. In 1969, he stated that 'we see the same process today in historic Asia and unhistoric Africa. In 1900 the colonial empires seemed "enlightened" ... The West was benevolent, cosmopolitan, the educator of the world.'[254] This 'unhistoric' Africa also included Egypt – perhaps the greatest of all early civilizations. It is indeed remarkable that even as late as the 1960s the rise and resilience of a civilization which constructed the largest pyramids on earth could still be described as belonging to a continent without historical development.

In a 1992 article 'The Trevor-Roper trap or the imperialism of history – an essay', Finn Fuglestad challenges the whole framework of Trevor-Roper's reasoning. According to Fuglestad, although Africanists have strongly criticized Trevor-Roper's position, they have seldom questioned his premises and chain of reasoning. Moreover, according to Fuglestad, many historians, while objecting to the premises, still fell into the trap set by Trevor-Roper through the dichotomy between 'civilized' and 'barbarian'; in other words, many Africanists allowed Trevor-Roper to define the 'rules of the game', squeezing African history into a Eurocentric straitjacket.[255]

It is not only history as a discipline that has a troublesome past with regard to studies and perceptions of Africa and Africans. Archaeology has also played a crucial role in creating these stereotypes of the African 'backward otherness'. As the archaeologist Bruce Trigger states: 'Colonialist archaeology ... served to denigrate native societies and peoples by trying to demonstrate that they had been static in prehistoric times and lacked the initiative to develop on their own.'[256] Consequently, 'While the colonisers had every reason to glorify their own past, they had no reason to extol the past of the peoples they were subjugating and supplanting. Indeed, they sought by emphasising the primitiveness and lack of accomplishments of these peoples to justify their own poor treatment of them.'[257]

Knowledge lacunae

One may rightly ask why it is necessary to repeat this history, when hopefully these traditions are gone forever and today's researchers work on different premises and within different paradigms. But these ideas were enunciated as recently as 50 years ago; and while their proponents may have gone, many of the implications and consequences remain. This relates to the decolonisation debates in Africa,[258] since:

> Africa is one of those epistemic sites that experienced not only colonial genocides but also 'theft of history' (...), epistemicides (killing of indigenous people's knowledges) and linguicides (killing of indigenous people's languages). Therefore, African

people's epistemic struggles are both old and new. They are old in the sense that they emerged at the very time of colonial encounters. They are new in the sense that they are re-emerging within a context of a deep present global systemic and epistemic crisis.[259]

Chilisa defines decolonisation this way:

> Decolonization is thus a process of conducting research in such a way that the worldviews of those who have suffered a long history of oppression and marginalization are given space to communicate from their frames of reference. It is a process that involves 'researching back' to question how the disciplines — psychology, education, history, anthropology, sociology, or science — through an ideology of Othering have described and theorized about the colonized Other, and refused to let the colonized Other name and know their frame of reference.[260]

Scientifically, 'Western enlightenment thought has [...] posited itself as the wellspring of universal learning, of Science and Philosophy [...],' the Comaroffs argue, 'it has regarded the non-West – variously known as the ancient, the orient, the primitive world, the third world, the underdeveloped world, the developing world, and now the global south — primarily as a place of parochial wisdom, of antiquarian traditions, of exotic ways and means.'[261] What is the role of African heritage as a resource for the future – in Africa and elsewhere?

Moreover, in a number of African countries, there is a knowledge lacuna when it comes to history and heritage. Also, the knowledge production and documentation are highly uneven. Egypt – the gift of the Nile since the time of the pharaohs – has been studied from time immemorial, and even the philosophers of antiquity were fascinated by the country. As Robert Wenke notes:

> Studies of ancient Egypt have become almost geologically encrusted with interpretations that draw on other interpretations that drew on earlier interpretations, and so on, reaching from the dynastic Egyptians themselves to classical Greek historians, and then century after century to the present day.[262]

As a tourist destination since the middle of the nineteenth century – and further inspired by the Agatha Christie notion of travelling on the Nile in a boat – the land of the pyramids has attracted scholars and tourists alike. In 1992, an American librarian documented 1,150 titles about journeys along the Nile – a veritable flood of books that continues to this day.[263]

Burundi, on the other hand, with a population of about 10 million (more or less the same as Sweden's), is a country about which few books have been written. The library at the Nordic Africa Institute in Uppsala is one of the best in Europe on Africa Studies, and it is one of the libraries with the most books on Burundi. Still, since 1966 (until March 2018) only 128 books have been catalogued under 'Burundi' (while the country may be mentioned in other books, these are not classified as books on Burundi; governmental prints/statistics are excluded).[264] If knowledge is important in development – not only knowledge of history and cultural heritage, but any knowledge about any societal processes in a country – then Burundi faces more challenges than most other countries. Of course, there might be other books on Burundi elsewhere; but visiting research scholars and students often stress that there are more books about their home countries in the big libraries abroad than they can find back home. In short, the knowledge lacuna represents huge challenges for development, since good development is dependent on good knowledge.

This relates to another aspect of the decolonization debate. More often than not, Western academics write academic articles and books; African researchers write consultancy reports. As Mkandawire points out: '… the academic community must support their counterparts in Africa as they struggle against the ravages of the consultancy syndrome that rewards reports over refereed academic papers, against the repressive practices and criminal negligence of their respective national governments and against the pressures for the commercialization of educational systems.'[265]

Another challenge or paradox is that much of the early history and ethnographic documentation is colonial in one way or another. John Hanning Speke arrived at the outlet of Lake Victoria, on the border between the Buganda and Busoga kingdoms, on 28 July 1862. He identified and defined this as the source of the White Nile (Figure 22).[266] Speke was the first to document these societies, and hence his books are the first

Figure 22. John Hanning Speke at Ripon Falls and the source of the White Nile, 28 July 1862. Painting at Speke Hotel, Kampala. Photo: Terje Oestigaard.

written accounts of the ethnography in this region. In the following decades, missionaries and colonial administrators documented other aspects, and John Roscoe's *The Baganda: An Account of Their Native Customs and Beliefs* from 1911 is an in-depth and important study of the traditions and beliefs at the turn of the twentieth century. In short, in Uganda, as elsewhere, much of the earliest documentation is done by explorers and missionaries, and later on by colonial administrators. Although much of this documentation is an invaluable source (and often remarkably accurate and scientific, by the standards of the day), it represents a paradox that independent countries have to rely on colonial accounts to reconstruct their history.

However, given that much of the indigenous knowledge has disappeared, one has to depend on early accounts for ethnographic description of nineteenth-century societies. In Kisumu in Kenya, it was pointed out in 1908: 'The native costume is unfortunately doomed to rapid disappearance. Here, as everywhere else, civilization, intolerant of all forms, aspects or traditions of life that differ from its own, is swiftly introducing that monotonous uniformity which tends to turn the whole world into one people.'[267] This directs the attention to another challenge: namely, the often-implicit practice of perceiving traditional customs as static and unchanged over the centuries. As Berry argues in *No Condition is Permanent*:

> 'traditions' did not necessarily stop changing when versions of them were written down, nor were debates over custom and social identity resolved, either during the colonial period or afterward. In general, the colonial period in Africa was less a time of transition – from isolation to global incorporation, from social equilibrium to turbulence, from collective solidarity to fragmented alienation – than an era of intensified condensation over custom, power and property.[268]

Thus, after this short detour in paradoxes and challenges, Berry's argument reminds us that traditions change because they matter, albeit in very different ways for the various actors. Hence, cultural heritage is a living heritage and tradition; and precisely for that reason it has relevance and importance today and in the future. Still, as Ingold points out, what seems to take place in the globalized world is 'the privileging of the global ontology of detachment over the local ontology of engagement'.[269] The local loses part of its importance, and it has been argued that local networks have 'increasingly been colonized or displaced by remote and more powerful networks'.[270] If this is correct, one returns to the poverty debate, where globalization and modernization processes are the drivers, and history and heritage are in the back seat. In short, not only African history but also the role of heritage needs a revival and strong focus, not least in a poverty and development perspective.

Research, relevance and returning to the rainbow and rainmaking

Traditional and indigenous religions and cultural practices are under severe pressure due to globalization and modernization. Mary Itanda complains that fewer and fewer people believe in the traditional religion and that they seldom conduct the appropriate and auspicious rites. Traditions often fade from history when the elders (or in this case the ritual specialists) die or disappear; and in the modern world it is difficult to convince enlightened youth that a sacrifice of a goat – or even a cow – can please the gods living in waterfalls and procure the life-giving rains (Figure 23).

Christians also condemn in various degrees the traditional practices as heresy or witchcraft, and in particular the Pentecostals see the healers and their practices as their arch enemies in the battle against evil. Then there are rumours of practices that existed in the past – and may, for all anybody knows, still exist – of human sacrifices at some of the waterfalls. The gods at Itanda Falls are not thirsty for human blood, and such rituals have never taken place at these falls – only charlatans and witchdoctors conduct human sacrifices, Mary said. What may have happened in the past at Bujagali Falls is another matter.[271] This emphasizes the fact that not all traditional practices were good; some are perhaps better left in the past. But it also raises important questions about what to do about troublesome pasts and heritages. Not everything is a source for the future, but the present cannot deny or erase pasts that have caused suffering and poverty to others.

In this Busoga case, with its emphasis on the traditional religion in general and the rainmaking cosmology in particular, there are strong external forces putting pressure on the belief systems, and thereby the heritage. And once a living tradition has been lost, it is almost impossible to revitalize. At best it may have been documented and could end up as a book on a shelf in a library (like this volume). While that has value in itself, it cannot be compared to a living tradition and heritage as active engagement in the present with the past for the benefit of the future.

Although there are religious conflicts between Christians and the traditional African religions, some Catholics in Jinja take another approach: they believe that the indigenous tradition is a rich resource for the future. The Cultural Research Centre in Jinja needs to be held up as an example to others. The centre is led by Rev. Richard K. Gonza, who, together with a team of assistants and ethnographers, is documenting as much as possible of the Busoga heritage. It is 'an institution under the Diocese of Jinja charged with the duty to research in, document, preserve and promote the culture of the Busoga. The Busoga are the natives of the big region, Busoga, in the eastern part of Uganda.'[272] They do a marvellous job documenting the ethnography of the Busoga, and I have derived great pleasure from their publications in my other studies.[273] Their vision is 'A harmonious, responsible and fully developed people that is deeply rooted in its cultural values and practices', and the principal objective is to 'research into, document, preserve and sensitise people about the culture of the Busoga, its relevance to society today'. Or in other words, development and prosperity have to build on culture and tradition.

Figure 23. The Itanda waterfalls. Photo: Terje Oestigaard.

With regard to research and studies of Africa, policy relevance is often stressed. In practice, this implies change or the view that current studies are a means to something else. While the aim of erasing economic poverty obviously implies change from prevailing conditions, the relevance of research may be quite different when it comes to the social and cultural dimensions of poverty – or cultural heritage in the broad sense. Moreover, within the policy world and poverty discourses, Africa often suffers from simplification and in many cases over-simplification. Simple solutions are sought to complex problems; or at least they are presented in this way, with short policy notes or recommendations with brief statements. This is not what Africa needs.

Relevance is an obvious and important criterion in any study, since researchers most often work using taxpayers' money. However, when it comes to the relevance of research in Africa, the relevance criteria need to be broadened, because a prime policy focus not only narrows African relevance, but also downplays African realities and heritages. What exists, in this case history and heritage, is very relevant, and hence a greater focus should be put on understanding culture and tradition.

Inevitably, the real world is complex and very complicated – indeed almost impossible to understand in many cases. By including and emphasizing the cultural and even the religious aspects of societies, the fuller complexity emerges; and while it may be frustrating from a simple policy perspective, which aims at quick fixes (or at least presumed quick fixes) on paper as part of poverty-mitigation discourses, this is the real reality from which changes have to happen and in which they are anchored. Thus, without understanding and acknowledging the complexity of cultures and societies, interventions for whatever purpose – even with the best of intentions – may jeopardize successful change, because they may not include people on their own terms. In other words, understanding complexity is an aim in itself, and any criteria of relevance are reduced by simplifying other people's lives and the challenges they face.

The lack of empirical documentation of African traditional religions and cultural heritage is striking, raising the question of how social and cultural sciences can best contribute to African developments. If social and cultural aspects of poverty are important issues, then the humanities can contribute significant knowledge in the long term. This is often very cost-effective as well, since the invaluable knowledge generated will last for generations and it is possible to conduct much work in the heritage sector without the need for large development organizations and institutions. Historical, ethnographic, anthropological and archaeological fieldwork and studies may generate immense knowledge, and these can often be conducted on an individual basis (except for archaeological excavations). Hence, a focus on the rich heritage is a good investment for the common future.

Given the colonial history and keeping the decolonisation debate in mind, an implicit or explicit emphasis on changing current conditions is problematic from a cultural and knowledge perspective: not only might it contribute to changing or erasing traditions, but it also seeks solutions to Africa's challenges elsewhere and abroad, rather than in indigenous cultures and heritage values. This is perhaps one of the main reasons why there is a greater need for a much stronger focus on cultural heritage and understanding the role of history – in this case the role of water in constituting society and religion. Successful changes must come from within, or at least be rooted in culture and tradition. All too often, external development processes have failed precisely because they are external and do not build on and incorporate the existing culture.

The rainbow and rainmaking do not in themselves solve current and future challenges, but the institutions they build on – anchored as they are in traditions and society – are sources of wealth. And most importantly, they are about the annual rains, on which everybody depends. Returning to religion and the Latin concept of religio (meaning 'binding together' or re-connect 'bonds' or 'relations') and socio (meaning 'compassion'),[274] one may better understand how and why religious practices are also intangible heritages, and, in this case, are manifested and visualized in the natural world and spectacular waterfalls. Apart from believing in the cosmological structure of the gods along the Nile, Mary Itanda emphasized precisely the social aspects of the rituals and the community that existed in the past. The rituals were obviously about religion; but it was also very much a social and community uniting activity.

Here, as elsewhere along this mighty river, 'the Nile is wealth'. Although angry gods and divine wrath are personal perceptions, the cosmology they define and work within are cultural frames, with a history spanning centuries or millennia. As a symbol, the rainbow has united people and has provided the life-giving rains; and even if the religious beliefs lose their importance in the future, it will remain a powerful symbol for coming generations, since it is an awe-inspiring sight. The waterfalls are part of the people's heritage, which includes culture and nature; hence it is a living tradition structured around all aspects of water. As the heritage of the past that builds and defines the future, nothing can be more important than life and the premises for life: water. Hence, water as heritage is a source for the future; and even though the traditional rainmaking ideology may change, the importance of river and rain will remain.

Literature

Anderson, S. 2001. Rejecting the rainbow Serpent: An Aboriginal Artist's Choice of the Christian God as Creator. *The Australian Journal of Anthropology*, 12(3): 291–301.

Aukema, J. 1989. Rain-making: a thousand year old ritual. *South African Archaeological Bulletin* 44: 70–72.

Auliya, M. et al. 2002. Review of the reticulated python (Python reticulatus Schneider, 1801) with the description of new subspecies from Indonesia. *Naturwissenschaften*. 2002 May; 89(5): 201–213.

Barker, D. G. et al. 2012. The Corrected Lengths of Two Well-known Giant Pythons and the Establishment of a New Maximum Length Record for Burmese Pythons, Python bivittatus. *Bull. Chicago Herp. Soc.* 47(1): 1–6.

Barnes, R. H. 1973. The Rainbow in the Representations of Inhabitants of the Flores Area of Indonesia. *Anthropos, Bd.* 68, H. 3/4: 611–613.

Barth, F. 1974. On Responsibility and Humanity: Calling a Colleague to Account. *Current Anthropology*, Vol. 15, No. 1: 99–103.

Barth, F. 1987 [1993]. *Cosmologies in the Making. A Generative Approach to Cultural Variation in Inner New Guinea.* Cambridge University Press. Cambridge.

Berry, S. 1993. *No Condition is Permanent. The Social Dynamics of Agrarian Change in Sub-Saharan Africa.* The University of Wisconsin Press. Wisconsin.

Bishop, R. L. & Newton, I. 1981. Rainbow over Woolsthorpe. *Notes and Records of the Royal Society of London*, Vol. 36, No. 1: 1–11.

Blust, R. 2000. The Origins of Dragons. *Anthropos, Bd.* 95, H. 2 (2000): 519–536.

Bourdieu, P. 1977. *Outline of a theory of practice.* Cambridge University Press. Cambridge.

Bourdieu, P. 1984. *Distinction: a social critique of the judgement of taste.* Harvard University Press. Cambridge, Mass.

Bourdieu, P. 1995. *The Logic of Practice.* Polity Press. Oxford.

Boyer, C. B. 1952. Descartes and the Radius of the Rainbow. *Isis*, Vol. 43, No. 2: 95–98.

Boyer, C. B. 1958a. The Tertiary Rainbow: An Historical Account. *Isis*, Vol. 49, No. 2: 141–154.

Boyer, C. B. 1958b. The Theory of the Rainbow: Medieval Triumph and Failure. *Isis*, Vol. 49, No. 4: 378–390.

Brumbaugh, R. 1987. The Rainbow Serpent on Upper Sepik. *Anthropos*, Bd. 82, H. 1/3: 25–33.

Brumfiel, E. M. 2003. It's A Material World: History, Artefacts, and Anthropology. *Annual Review of Anthropology*, Vol. 32(2003): 205–223.

Byerley, A. 2005. *Becoming Jinja. The Production of Space and Making of Place in and African Industrial Town.* Department of Human Geography. Stockholm University. Stockholm.

Carrasco, D. 1999. *City of Sacrifice. The Aztec Empire and the Role of Violence in Civilization.* Beacon Press. Boston.

Chilisa, B. 2012. *Indigenous Research Methodologies. Sage.* Los Angeles/London/New Delhi.

Comaroff, J. & Comaroff, J. L. 2012. *Theory From the South Or, How Euro-America Is Evolving Toward Africa.* Paradigm Publishers. Boulder and London.

Daes, E. I. 1993. *Study on the Protection of the Cultural and Intellectual Property of Indigenous Peoples.* United Nations. New York.

Dawkins, R. 1998. *Unweaving the Rainbow. Science, Delusion and the Appetite for Wonder.* Houghton Mifflin. Boston, Massachusetts.

Dickow, H. & Møller, V. 2002. South Africa's "Rainbow People", National Pride and Optimism: A Trend Study. *Social Indicators Research*, Vol. 59, No. 2: 175–202.

Dowson, T. A. 1993. Rain in Bushman belief, politics and history; the rock-art of rain-making in the southeastern mountains, southern Africa. In Chippendale, C. and Taçon, P.S.C. (eds.). *The archaeology of Rock-Art*: 73–89. University of Cambridge Press. Cambridge.

Drewal, J. H. 1988a. Mermaids, Mirrors, and Snake Charmers: Igbo Mami Wata Shrines. *African Arts*, Vol. 21, No. 2: 38–45+96.

Drewal, J. H. 1988b. Performing the Other: Mami Wata Worship in Africa. *TDR*, Vol. 32, No. 2: 160–185.

Eliade, M. 1973. *Australian Religions: An Introduction.* Cornell University Press. Ithaca, New York.

Eliade, M. 1993. *Patterns in Comparative Religion.* Sheed and Ward Ltd. London.

Elster, J. 1987. *Making Sense of Marx.* Cambridge University Press. Cambridge.

Elster, J. 1989. *The Cement of Society. A Study of Social Order.* Cambridge. University Press. Cambridge.

Epstein, J. L. & Greenberg, M. L. 1984. Decomposing Newton's Rainbow. *Journal of the History of Ideas*, Vol. 45, No. 1: 115–140.

Erlich, H. & Gershoni, I. 2000. Introduction. In Erlich, H. & Gershoni, I. (eds.). *The Nile: Histories, Cultures, Myths*: 1–14. Lynne Rienner Publishers. Boulder, CO and London.

Fage, J. D. 1978. Introduction. In Fage, J. D. & Oliver, R. (eds.). *The Cambridge History of Africa.* Volume 2. From c. 500 BC to AD 1050: 1–10. Cambridge University Press. Cambridge.

Fage, J. D. & Oliver, R. 1978. Preface. In Fage, J. D. & Oliver, R. (eds.). *The Cambridge History of Africa.* Volume 2. From c. 500 BC to AD 1050: xiv–xvi. Cambridge University Press. Cambridge.

Faherty, R. L. 1974. *Sacrifice.* The New Encyclopaedia Britannica. 15th ed. Macropaedia. Vol. 16: 128–135.

Falola, T. 2002. Introduction. In Falola, T. (ed.). *Africa Vol. 3. Colonial Africa, 1885–1939:* xvii– xxiii. Carolina Academic Press. Durham, North Carolina.

Filippi, F. de. 1908. Ruwenzori. *An account of the expedition of H.R.H. Prince Luigi Amedeo of Savoy duke of the Abruzzi.* Archibald Constable and Company Limited. London.

Finlay, R. 2007. Weaving the Rainbow: Visions of Color in World History. *Journal of World History*, Vol. 18, No. 4: 383–431.

Fisher, P. 1998. *Wonder, The Rainbow, and the Aesthetics of Rare Experiences.* Harvard University Press. Cambridge.

Fuglestad, F. 1992. The Trevor-Roper Trap or the Imperialism of History. An Essay. *History in Africa*, Vol. 19: 309–326.

Galaty, J. G. 1984. *Review The Drunken King or the Origin of the State* by Luc De Heusch and Roy Willis. *American Ethnologist*, Vol. 11, No. 3: 603–604.

Giddens, A. 1979. *Central problems in social theory: action, structure and contradiction in social analysis.* University of California Press. Berkeley.

Giddens, A. 1987. *Social theory and modern sociology. Polity in association with Blackwell.* Cambridge.

Giddens, A. 1989. *Sociology.* Polity Press. Cambridge.

Giddens, A. 1993. *The Constitution of Society.* Polity Press. Cambridge.

Giddens, A. 1999. Risk and Responsibility. *The Modern Law Review.* Vol. 62, No. 1: 1-10.

Gigante, D. 2002. The Monster in the Rainbow: Keats and the Science of Life. *PMLA*, Vol. 17, No. 3: 433–448.

Gilje, N. & Grimen, H. 2001. *Samfunnsvitenskapenes forutsetninger. Innføring i samfunnsviten-skapenes vitenskapsfilosofi.* Universitetsforlaget. Oslo.

Glazier, J. 1984. *Review The Drunken King, or the Origin of the State* by Luc de Heusch and Roy Willis. *The Journal of American Folklore*, Vol. 97, No. 383: 71–73.

Goethe, J. W. 1840. *Goethe's Theory of Colours.* Translated from the German: with notes by Charles Lock Eastlake. John Murray. London.

Goody, J. 1986. *The Logic of Writing and the Organisation of Society.* Cambridge University Press. Cambridge.

Gonza, R. K. et al. 2001. *Reconciliation among the Busoga.* Cultural Research Centre. Jinja.

Gonza, R. K. et al. 2002. *Traditional Religion and Clans Among the Busoga.* Vol. 1. Cultural Research Centre. Jinja.

Gonza, R. K. et al. 2003. *Witchcraft, Divination and Healing among the Basoga.* Cultural Research Centre. Jinja.

Gonza, R. K. et al. 2010. *The Concept of Good Luck and Bad Luck among the Basoga.* Marianum Publishing Company. Kisubi.

Gorman, R. 1982. *Neo-Marxism. The Meanings of Modern Radicalism.* Greenwood Press. London.

Hambly, W. D. 1929. The Serpent in African Belief and Custom. *American Anthropologist*, New Series, Vol. 31, No. 4: 655–666.

Hegel, G. W. F. 2007[1899]. *The Philosophy of History.* Cosimo. New York.

Heien, K. H. 2007. *Local Livelihoods and the Bujagali Hydro-Power Dam, Uganda.* MA-thesis. Faculty of Economics and Social Sciences. Agder University College. Kristiansand.

Heine, B. 1985. The Mountain People: Some Notes on the Ik of North-eastern Uganda. *Africa: Journal of the International African Institute*, Vol. 55, No. 1: 3-16.

Herskovits, M. 1945. The process of cultural change. In Linton, R. (ed.). *The science of man in world crisis*. Columbia University Press. New York.

Heusch, L. de. 1982. *The Drunken King or the Origin of the State*. Translated and annotated by Roy Willis. Indiana University Press. Bloomington.

Hobley, C. W. 1929. *Kenya: From Chartered Company to Crown Colony. Thirty years of exploration and administration in British East Africa*. H.F. & G. Witherby. London.

Hoff, A. 1997. The water Snake of the Khoekhoen and /Xam. *The South African Archaeological Bulletin*, Vol. 52, No. 165: 21–37.

Holmberg, U. 1916. *The Mythology of All Races*, Vol. 4. Finno-Ugric, Siberian. Archaeological Institute of America. Boston.

Holtorf, C. and Högberg, A. 2015. Contemporary Heritage and the Future. In Waterton, E. and Watson, S. (eds.). *The Palgrave Handbook of Contemporary Heritage Research*: 509–523. Palgrave Macmillan. Basingstoke.

Hopkins, L. C. 1931. Where the Rainbow Ends (An Introduction to the Dragon Terrestrial and the Dragon Celestial). *The Journal of the Royal Asiatic Society of Great Britain and Ireland*, No. 3: 603–612.

Hubert, H. & Mauss, M. 1964. *Sacrifice: Its Nature and Function*. The University of Chicago Press. Chicago.

Hughes-Hallett, P. 2002. *The Mystery of the Rainbow*. New England Review, Vol. 23, No. 4: 131–145.

Human Development Report 2006. *Beyond scarcity: Power, poverty and the global water crisis*. UNDP. New York.

Högberg, A., Holtorf, C., May, S. & Wollentz, G. 2017. No future in archaeological heritage management?, *World Archaeology*, 49:5, 639–647, DOI: 10.1080/00438243.2017.1406398

Hårsmar, M. 2016. Misconceptions and Poor Understanding. The Debate on Poverty. In Havnevik, K., Oestigaard, T., Virtanen, T. & Tobisson, E. (eds.). 2016. *Framing African Development. Challenging Concepts*: 35–61. Brill. Leiden.

Ingersoll, E. 1928. *Dragons and Dragon Lore*. Payson and Clarke. New York.

Ingold, T. 2000. *The Perception of the Environment*. Routledge. London.

Insoll, T. 2004. Are Archaeologists Afraid of Gods? Some Thoughts on Archaeology and Religion. In Insoll, T. (ed.). *Belief in the Past. The Proceedings of the Manchester Conference on Archaeology and Religion*: 1–6. BAR International Series 1212. Oxford.

Insoll, T. 2005. Archaeology of Cult and Religion. In Renfrew, C. and Bahn, P. (eds.). *Archaeology: The Key Concepts*: 45–49. Routledge. London.

Jacobi, J. 1951. *The Psychology of C. G. Jung: An Introduction with Illustrations*. Routledge. London.

Jacobi, J. 1959. *Complex/Archetype/Symbol in the psychology of C. G. Jung.* Routledge and Kegan Paul. London.

Johnson, P. 2007. Proof of the Heavenly Iris: The Fountain of Three Rainbows at Wilton House, Wiltshire. *Garden History*, Vol. 35, No. 1: 51–67.

Jones, O. and Cloke, P. 2002. *Three Cultures.* Berg. Oxford.

Jung, C. G. 1959. Forward. In Jacobi, J. *Complex/Archetype/Symbol. In the psychology of C. G. Jung:* ix–xi. Routledge and Kegan Paul. London.

Jung, C. G. 1968a. *The Psychology of the Child Archetype.* In The Archetypes and the Collective Unconscious. The Collected Works Volume 9, Part 1: 151–181. Routledge and Kegan Paul. London.

Jung, C. G. 1968b. *Concerning the Archetypes, with Special Reference to the Anima Concept.* In The Archetypes and the Collective Unconscious. The Collected Works Volume 9, Part 1: 54–74. Routledge and Kegan Paul. London.

Jung, C. G. 1968c. *Psychological Aspects of the Mother Archetype.* In The Archetypes and the Collective Unconscious. The Collected Works Volume 9, Part 1: 75–110. Routledge and Kegan Paul. London.

Kenny, M. G. 1977. The Powers of Lake Victoria. *Anthropos*, Bd. 72, H. 5/6: 717–733.

Knight, J. 1994. 'The Mountain People' as Tribal Mirror. *Anthropology Today*, Vol. 10, No. 6: 1–3.

Kodesh, N. 2007. History from the Healer's Shrine: Genre, Historical Imagination, and Early Ganda History. *Comparative Studies in Society and History,* Vol. 49, No. 3: 527–552.

Krokfors, C. 1995. Poverty, Environmental Stress and Culture as factors in African Migrations. In Baker, J. & Aida, T. A. (eds.). *The Migration Experience in Africa:* 54–64. The Nordic Africa Institute. Uppsala.

Lan, D. 1985. *Guns and rain: guerillas and spirit mediums in Zimbabwe.* James Currey ltd. London.

Latour, B. 1993. *We Have Never Been Modern.* Prentice Hall. London.

Latour, B. 1997. The Trouble with Actor-Network Theory. *Philosophia.* Vol. 25, No. 3–4: 47–64.

Latour, B. 1999. *Pandora's Hope. Essays on the Reality of Science Studies.* Harvard University Press. Cambridge, MA.

Latour, B. 2003. Revolution. In Pepper, D., et al. (eds.). *Environmentalism. Critical Concepts.* Vol. V: 287–327. Routledge. London.

Leclerc, I. 2014. *The Nature of Physical Existence.* Routledge. London.

Lee, R. L, Jr. & Fraser, A. B. 2001. *The Rainbow Bridge. Rainbows in Art, Myth, and Science.* The Pennsylvania State University Press. Pennsylvania.

Lefebvre, H. 1997. The Production of Space. In Leach, N. (ed.). *Rethinking Architecture. A reader in cultural theory:* 139–147. Routledge. London.

Lévi-Strauss, C. 1969. *The Raw and the Cooked.* The University of Chicago Press. Chicago.

Lewis, O. 1966. *La vida: a Puerto Rican family in the culture of poverty – San Juan and New York.* Random House. New York.

Lewis, O. 1967. Reviewed Works: *The Children of Sánchez: Autobiography of a Mexican Family by Oscar Lewis; Pedro Martínez: A Mexican Peasant and His Family by Oscar Lewis; La Vida: A Puerto Rican Family in the Culture of Poverty by Oscar Lewis.* Current Anthropology 8, no. 5, Part 1 (Dec., 1967): 480–500.

Lewis-Williams, D. 1977. Led by the nose: observations on the supposed use of southern San rock art in rain-making rituals. *African studies* 36: 155–159.

Lindberg, D. C. 1966. Roger Bacon's Theory of the Rainbow: Progress or Regress? *Isis*, Vol. 57, No. 2: 235–248.

Lissmann, H. W. 1950. Rectilinear Locomotion in a Snake (Boa Occidentalis). *Journal of Experimental Biology* 1950 26: 368–379.

Lorberbaum, Y. 2009. The Rainbow in the Cloud: An Anger-Management Device. *The Journal of Religio*n, Vol. 89, No. 4: 498–540.

Lucas, G. 1995. Interpretation in contemporary archaeology: some philosophical issues. In Hodder, I. et al. (eds.). *Interpreting archaeology: Finding meaning in the past*: 37–44. Routledge. London.

Lurker, M. 2005. Snakes. In *Encyclopedia of Religion*, Vol. 12: 8456–8460. Second Edition. Thomson Gale. Detroit.

Lœwenstein, J. 1961. Rainbow and Serpent. *Anthropos*, Bd. 56, H. 1./2. (1961): 31–40.

Marx, K. 1970. *A contribution to the critique of political economy.* International Publishers. New York.

Melber, H. 2018. Knowledge production and decolonisation – Not only African challenges. *Strategic Review for Southern Africa*, Vol. 40, No. 1: 4–15.

Meserve, H. C. 1987. Editorial: Searching for the Rainbow's End. *Journal of Religion and Health*, Vol. 26, No. 1: 3–8.

Miller, D. 1985. *Artefacts as Categories: A Study of Ceramic Variability in Central India.* Cambridge University Press. Cambridge.

Miller, D. 1987. *Material Culture and Mass Consumption.* Basil Blackwell. Oxford.

Miller, D. 1994. Artefacts and the meaning of things. In Ingold, T. (ed.) *Companion encyclopedia of anthropology*:. 396–419. Routledge. London.

Miller, D. 1998. Introduction: Why some things matter. In Miller, D. (ed.). *Material cultures – Why some things matter*: 3–21. University College London Press. London.

Miller, D. & Tilley, C. 1996. Editorial. *Journal of Material Culture* Vol. 1, No. 1: 5–14.

Mkandawire, T. 2002. "African Intellectuals, Political Culture and Development". *Austrian Journal of Development Studies*, Vol. 18, No. 1: 31–47.

M'Kenzie, D. 1907. Children and Wells. *Folklore*, Vol. 18, No. 3: 253–282.

Modéus, M. 2005. *Sacrifice and Symbol. Biblical Šĕlāmîm in a Ritual Perspective.* Coniectanea Biblica Old Testament Series 52. Almquist and Wiksell International. Stockholm.

Mountford, C. P. 1956. *Art, Myth and Symbolism: Records of the American – Australian Expedition to Arnhem Land,* Vol. 1. Melbourne University Press. Melbourne.

Mundkur, B. 1978. The Roots of Ophidian Symbolism. *Ethos,* Vol. 6, No. 3: 125–158.

Murphy, J. C. & Henderson, R. W. 1997. *Tales of Giant Snakes. A Natural History of Anacondas and Pythons.* Krieger Publishing Company. Malabar, Florida.

Ndlovu-Gatsheni, S. J. 2018. The Dynamics of Epistemological Decolonisation in the 21st Century: Towards Epistemic Freedom. *Strategic Review for Southern Africa,* Vol. 40, No. 1: 16–45.

Newton, I. 1704. *Opticks: or, a treatise of the reflexions, refractions, inflexions and colours of light. Also two treatises of the species and magnitude of curvilinear figures.* Sam Smith & Benj. Walford. London.

Nhamo, A. Saetersdal, T. & Walderhaug, E. 2007. *Ancestral Landscapes. Reporting on Rock Art in the border regions between Zimbabwe and Mozambique.* In: Zimbabwea, Special Issue, Number 9. National Museums and Monuments of Zimbabwe. Harare.

Nussenzveig, H. M. 1977. The Theory of the Rainbow. *Scientific American,* 236: 116–127.

Nyamnjoh, F. 2016. #RhodesMustFall: *Nibbling at Resilient Colonialism in South Africa.* Langaa. Bamenda.

Oestigaard, T. 2003. *An Archaeology of Hell: Fire, Water and Sin in Christianity.* Bricoleur Press. Lindome.

Oestigaard, T. 2005. *Water and World Religions. An Introduction.* SFU & SMR. Bergen.

Oestigaard, T. 2008. The Sisters Kali and Ganga: Waters of Life and Death. In Håland, E. (ed.). *Women, Pain and Death: Rituals and Everyday Life on the Margins of Europe and Beyond:* 203–221. Cambridge Scholars Publishing. Newcastle upon Tyne.

Oestigaard, T. (ed.). 2009. *Water, Culture and Identity. Comparing Past and Present Traditions in the Nile Basin Region.* BRIC Press. Bergen.

Oestigaard, T. 2010. Purification, Purgation and Penalty: Christian Concepts of Water and Fire in Heaven and Hell. In Tvedt, T. & Oestigaard, T. (eds.). *A History of Water. Series 2, Vol. 1. The Ideas of Water from Antiquity to Modern Times:* 298–322. I.B. Tauris. London.

Oestigaard, T. 2011. Water. In Insoll, T. (ed.). *The Oxford Handbook of the Archaeology of Ritual and Religion:* 38–50. Oxford University Press. Oxford.

Oestigaard, T. 2014. *Religion at Work in Globalised Traditions. Rainmaking, Witchcraft and Christianity in Tanzania.* Cambridge Scholars Publishing. Newcastle.

Oestigaard, T. 2015. *Dammed Divinities. The Water Powers at Bujagali Falls, Uganda.* Current African Issues No. 62. The Nordic Africa Institute. Uppsala.

Oestigaard, T. 2016. Developing the 'Other' – Challenging Concepts. In Havnevik, K., Oestigaard, T., Tobisson, E. & Virtanen, T. 2016 (eds.). *Framing African Development. Challenging Concepts:* 16–34. Brill. Leiden.

Oestigaard, T. 2018. *The Religious Nile. Water, Ritual and Society since Ancient Egypt.* I.B. Tauris. London.

Oestigaard, T. in press. Waterfalls and moving waters: the unnatural natural and flows of cosmic forces. In Day, J. and Skeates, R. (eds.). *Routledge Handbook of Sensory Archaeology.* Routledge. London.

Oestigaard, T. & Gedef, A. F. 2013. *The Source of the Blue Nile – Water Rituals and Traditions in the Lake Tana Region.* Cambridge Scholars Publishing. Newcastle.

Oyebade, A. 2000. The Study of Africa in Historical Perspective. In Falola, T. (ed.). *Africa. Vol. 1. African History Before 1885:* 7–22. Carolina Academic Press. Durham, North Carolina.

Pope, C. 1961. *The Giant Snakes. The Natural History of the Boa Constrictor, the Anaconda, and the largest Pythons, including comparative facts about other snakes and basic information about reptiles in general.* Routledge and Kegan Paul. London.

Radcliffe-Brown, A. R. 1926. The Rainbow-Serpent Myth of Australia. *The Journal of the Royal Anthropological Institute of Great Britain and Ireland,* Vol. 56: 19–25.

Read, K. A. 1998. *Time and sacrifice in the Aztec Cosmos.* Indiana University Press. Bloomington.

Riley, C. A 1995. *Color Codes. Modern Theories of Color in Philosophy, Painting and Architecture, Literature, Music, and Psychology.* University Press of New England. Hanover and London.

Rodis-Lewis, G. 1998. *Descartes. His Life and Thoughts.* Cornell University Press. Ithaca and London.

Roscoe, J. 1909. Python Worship in Uganda. *Man,* Vol. 9 (1909): 88–90.

Roscoe, J. 1911. *The Baganda. An Account of Their Native Customs and Beliefs.* Macmillan and Co. London.

Saetersdal, T. 2009. Manica Rock-Art in Contemporary Society. In Oestigaard, T. (ed.). 2009. *Water, Culture and Identity. Comparing Past and Present Traditions in the Nile Basin Region:* 55–82. BRIC Press. Bergen.

Saetersdal, T. 2010. Rain, Snakes and Sex – Making Rain: Rock Art and Rain-making in Africa and America. In Tvedt, T. & Oestigaard, T. (eds.). 2010. *A History of Water. Series 2, Vol. 1. Ideas of Water from Antiquity to Modern Times:* 378–404. I.B. Tauris. London.

Sanders, T. 2008. *Beyond Bodies. Rainmaking and Sense Making in Tanzania.* Toronto University Press. Toronto.

Sarapik, V. 1998. Rainbow, Colours and Science Mythology. *Folklore 6:* 7–19.

Sarton, G. 1952. *Ancient Science Through the Golden Age of Greece.* Dover Publications, Inc. New York.

Schapera, I. 1971. *Rain-making rites of Tswana tribes.* African Social Research Documents – Volume 3, African studies centre, Cambridge.

Schebesta, P. 1950. *Die Bambuti-Pygmäen vom Ituri.* Roy. Colonial Belge 2. Brussels.

Schmidt, I. 1979. The Rain Bull of the South African Bushmen. *African Studies* Vol. 38: 201–224.

Schoeman, M. H. 2006. Imagining rain-places: Rain-control and changing ritual landscapes in the Shashe-Limpopo Confluence Area, South Africa. *The South African Archaeological Bulletin*, Vol 61. Number 184: 152–165.

Schweizer, P. D. 1982. John Constable, Rainbow Science, and English Color Theory. *The Art Bulletin*, Vol. 64, No. 3: 424–445.

Shine, R. et al. 1998. The Influence of Sex and Body Size on Food Habits of a Giant Tropical Snake, Python reticulatus. *Functional Ecology*, Vol. 12, No. 2: 248–258.

Skarstein, R. 2016. Primitive Accumulation: Concept, Similarities and Varieties. In Havnevik, K., Oestigaard, T., Virtanen, T. & Tobisson, E. (eds.). *Framing African Development. Challenging Concepts*: 135–168. Brill. Leiden.

Small, M.L., Harding, D.J. & Lamont, M. 2010. Reconsidering Culture and Poverty. Introduction. *The Annals of the American Academy, AAPSS*, 629: 5–27.

Smith, E. W. 1952. African Symbolism. *The Journal of the Royal Anthropological Institute of Great Britain and Ireland*, Vol. 82, No. 1: 13–37.

Sontum, K. H. & Fredriksen, P. D. 2018. When The Past is slipping. Value tensions and responses by heritage management to demographic changes: a case study from Oslo, Norway. *International Journal of Heritage Studies*, Vol. 24, No. 4: 406–420.

Speke, J. H. 1863. *Journal of the Discovery of the Source of the White Nile.* Blackwood and Sons. Edinburgh and London.

Speke, J. H. 1864. *What Led to the Discovery of the Source of the Nile.* Blackwood and Sons. Edinburgh and London.

Staniland Wake, C. 1873. The Origin of Serpent-Worship. *The Journal of the Anthropological Institute of Great Britain and Ireland*, Vol. 2(1873): 373–390.

Starin, E. & Burghardt, G. M. 1982. African rock pythons Python sebae in the Gambia observations on natural history and interactions with Primates. *Snake.* August; 241: 50–62.

Stillinger, J. (ed.). 1978. *The Poems of John Keats.* Part II. Cambridge. Massachusetts.

Stothers, R. B. 2004. Ancient Scientific Basis of the "Great Serpent" from Historical Evidence. *Isis*, Vol. 95, No. 2 (June 2004): 220–238.

Struhsaker, T. T. 1997. *Ecology of an African rain forest. Logging in Kibale and the Conflict between Conservation and Exploitation.* University of Florida Press. Gainesville.

Taçon, P. S. C. 1991. The power of stone: symbolic aspects of stone use and tool development in western Arnhem Land, Australia. *Antiquity* 65 (1991): 192–207.

Taçon, P. S. C., Wilson, M. & Chippindale, C. 1996. Birth of the rainbow Serpent in Arnhem Land rock art and oral history. *Archaeology in Oceania*, Vol. 31: 103-124.

Taçon, P. S. C. 2008. Rainbow colour and power among the Waanyis of Northwest Queensland. *Cambridge Archaeological Journal* 18(2): 163-176.

Taylor, L. 1990. The Rainbow Serpent as visual metaphor in western Arnhem Land. *Oceania* 60: 329–44.

Taylor, L. 2008. 'They May Say Tourist, May Say Truly Painting': Aesthetic Evolution and Meaning of Bark Paintings in Western Arnhem Land, Northern Australia. *The Journal of the Royal Anthropological Institute*, Vol. 14, No. 4: 865–885.

Taylor, L. 2012. *Connections of Spirit: Kuninjku Attachments to Country.* In Weir, J. K. (ed.). *Country, Native Title and Ecology*: 21–45. ANU Press. Canberra.

Thankappan Nair, P. 1974. The Peacock Cult in Asia. *Asian Folklore Studies*, Vol. 33, No. 2: 93–170.

Trevor-Roper, H. 1965. *The Rise of Christian Europe.* Thames and Hudson. London.

Trevor-Roper, H. 1969. The Past and the Present. History and Sociology. *The Past and Present Society*, No. 42: 3–17.

Trigger, B. 1984. Archaeologies: Nationalist, Colonialist, Imperialist. *Man*, New Series, Vol. 19, No. 3: 355–370.

Tshimanga, R. M. 2009. Traditional Values and Uses of Water along the upper Congo River. In Oestigaard, T. (ed.). *Water, Culture and Identity. Comparing Past and Present Traditions in the Nile Basin Region*: 21–51. BRIC Press. Bergen.

Tshimanga, R. M. 2010. *Traditional Systems of Water and water Resources Management along the Upper Congo River.* Fountain Publishers. Kampala.

Tshimanga, R. M. 2016. Water and food systems in the Congo rainforest. In Tvedt, T. & Oestigaard, T. (eds.). *A History of Water, Series 3, Vol. 3. Water and Food: From hunter-gatherers to global production in Africa:* 355–368. I.B. Tauris. London.

Todd, L. 1984. Review *The Drunken King, or, the Origin of the State* by Luc de Heusch and Roy Willis. Folklore, Vol. 95, No. 1: 129–130.

Turnbull, C. 1961. *The Forest People.* Simon and Schuster. New York.

Turnbull, C. M. 1972[1987]. *The Mountain People.* Simon & Schuster. New York.

Turner, B. 1991. *Religion and Social Theory.* Sage. London.

Turner, L. A. 1993. The Rainbow as the Sign of the Covenant in the Genesis IV 11–13. *Vetus Testamentum*, Vol. 43, Fasc. 1 (Jan., 1993): 119–124.

Tvedt, T. 2004. *The River Nile in the Age of the British. Political Ecology and the Quest for Economic Power.* I.B. Tauris. London.

Tvedt, T. 2010a. Why England and not China and India? Water systems and the history of the industrial revolution. *Journal of Global History* Vol. 5: 29–50.

Tvedt, T. 2010b. Water: a source of wars or a pathway to peace? An empirical critique of two dominant schools of thought on water and international politics. In Tvedt, T., Chapman, G. & Hagen, R. (eds). *A History of Water, Series 3, Vol. 3 Water, Geopolitics and the New World Order*: 78–108. I.B.Tauris. London.

Tvedt, T. 2010c. Water systems, environmental history and the deconstruction of nature, *Environment and History*, Vol. 16: 143–66.

Tvedt, T. 2011. Hydrology and empire: The Nile, water imperialism and the partition of Africa. *The Journal of Imperial and Commonwealth History*, Vol. 39, No. 2: 173–94.

Tvedt, T. 2012. *Nilen – historiens elv.* Aschehoug. Oslo.

Tvedt, T. 2016. *Water and Society – Changing Perceptions of Societal and Historical Development.* I.B.Tauris. London.

Tvedt, T. & Oestigaard, T. 2016. Approaches to African Food Production in a Water Society Systems Perspective. In Tvedt, T. & Oestigaard, T. (eds.). *A History of Water, Series 3, Volume 3. Water and Food: From Hunter-Gatherers to Global Production in Africa*: 1–25. I.B. Tauris. London.

Tylor, E. B. 1958[1871]. *Primitive Culture 2. Religion in primitive culture.* New York.

Underhill, E. 1912. *Mysticism. A study in the nature and development of man's spiritual consciousness.* Dutton. New York.

Vaidya, P. B. & Amtzis, W. 1996/1997. Water is water. *Journal of South Asian Literature,* Vol. 31/32, No. 1/2: 208.

Valeri, V. 1985. *Kingship and Sacrifice. Ritual and Society in Ancient Hawaii.* The University Press of Chicago. Chicago.

Wang, E. Y. 2005. *Mirror, Moon, and Memory in Eighth-Century China: From Dragon Pond to Lunar Palace.* Cleveland Studies in the History of Art, Vol. 9 (Clarity and Luster: New Light on Bronze Mirrors in tang and Post-Tang Dynasty China, 600–1300: Papers from a Symposium on the Carter Collection of Chinese Bronze Mirrors at the Cleveland Museum of Art): 42–67.

Watkins, J. W. N. 1973. Ideal types and historical explanation. In Ryan, A. (ed.). *The Philosophy of Social Explanation.* Oxford University Press. Oxford.

Weissenborn, J. 1906a. Animal-Worship in Africa. *Journal of the Royal African Society,* Vol. 5, No. 18: 167–181.

Weissenborn, J. 1906b. Animal-Worship in Africa (Concluded from p. 181). *Journal of the Royal African Society,* Vol. 5, No. 18: 269–289.

Wenke, R. 2009. *The Ancient Egyptian State: The Origins of Egyptian Culture* (c. 8000–2000 bc). Cambridge University Press. Cambridge.

Werrett, S. 2001. Wonders Never Cease: Descartes's "Métores" and the Rainbow Fountain. *The British Journal for the History of Science,* Vol. 34, No. 2: 129–147.

Wessing, R. 2006. Symbolic Animals in the Land between Waters: Markers of Place and Transition. *Asian Folklore Studies,* Vol. 65, No. 2: 205–239.

Whitehead, A. N. 1927. *Religion in the Making. Cambridge at the University Press.* Cambridge.

Wittgenstein, L. 1972. *Philosophical Investigations,* edited by Anscombe, G. E. M & von Wright, G. H. Blackwell. Oxford.

Witzel, M. 2015. Water in Mythology. *Dædalus, the Journal of the American Academy of Arts & Sciences*: 18–26.

Worms, E. A. 1955. Contemporary and Prehistoric Rock Paintings in Central and Northern Kimberley. *Anthropos,* Bd. 50, H. 4/6: 546–566.

Wrigley, C. 1988. The River-God and the Historians. Myth in the Shire Valley and Elsewhere. *The Journal of African History,* Vol. 29, No. 3: 267–383.

Endnotes

1   Lee, R. L, Jr. & Fraser, A. B. 2001. *The Rainbow Bridge. Rainbows in Art, Myth, and Science.* The Pennsylvania State University Press. Pennsylvania, p. vii.

2   See Oestigaard, T. 2015. *Dammed Divinities. The Water Powers at Bujagali Falls, Uganda.* Current African Issues No. 62. The Nordic Africa Institute. Uppsala; Oestigaard, T. 2018. *The Religious Nile. Water, Ritual and Society since Ancient Egypt.* I.B. Tauris. London.

3   Oestigaard 2018:224.

4   https://www.un.org/sustainabledevelopment/cities/ (accessed 6 April 2018)

5   http://www.unesco.org/new/en/social-and-human-sciences/themes/international-migration/glossary/poverty/ (accessed 5 April 2018)

6   http://www.unesco.org/new/en/culture/themes/culture-and-development/the-future-we-want-the-role-of-culture/poverty-alleviation/ (accessed 5 April 2018)

7   http://www.unesco.org/new/en/culture/themes/culture-and-development/ (accessed 5 April 2018)

8   http://www.unesco.org/new/en/culture/themes/illicit-trafficking-of-cultural-property/unesco-database-of-national-cultural-heritage-laws/frequently-asked-questions/definition-of-the-cultural-heritage/ (Assessed 9 April 2018)

9   Number B-0130-UG, Indemnity Agreement (Partial Risk Guarantee for the Private Power Generation (Bujagali) Project) between International Development Association and Republic of Uganda. Dated July 18, 2007.

10   Tylor, E. B. 1958[1871]. *Primitive Culture 2. Religion in primitive culture.* New York.

11   Mexico City Declaration on Cultural Policies, World Conference on Cultural Policies, Mexico City, 26 July – 6 August 1982. http://portal.unesco.org/culture/en/files/35197/11919410061mexico_en.pdf/mexico_en. pdf (Accessed 28 May 2012).

12   Herskovits, M. 1945. The process of cultural change. In Linton, R. (ed.). *The science of man in world crisis.* Columbia University Press. New York, p. 158.

13   Daes, E. I. 1993. *Study on the Protection of the Cultural and Intellectual Property of Indigenous Peoples.* United Nations. New York, p. 8.

14   See Hårsmar, M. 2016. Misconceptions and Poor Understanding. The Debate on Poverty. In Havnevik, K., Oestigaard, T., Virtanen, T. & Tobisson, E. (eds.). *Framing African Development. Challenging Concepts:* 35–61. Brill. Leiden.

15   Lewis, O. 1966. *La vida: a Puerto Rican family in the culture of poverty – San Juan and New York.* Random House. New York.

16   Giddens, A. 1979. *Central problems in social theory: action, structure and contradiction in social analysis.* University of California Press. Berkeley; Giddens, A. 1987. *Social theory and modern sociology.* Polity in association with Blackwell. Cambridge; Giddens, A. 1989. *Sociology.* Polity Press. Cambridge; Giddens, A. 1993. *The Constitution of Society.* Polity Press. Cambridge.

17   Small, M.L., Harding, D.J. & Lamont, M. 2010. Reconsidering Culture and Poverty. Introduction. *The Annals of the American Academy,* AAPSS, 629: 5–27, p. 7.

18   Lewis, O. 1967. Reviewed Works: *The Children of Sánchez: Autobiography of a Mexican Family* by Oscar Lewis; Pedro Martínez: *A Mexican Peasant and His Family* by Oscar Lewis; *La Vida: A Puerto Rican Family in the Culture of Poverty* by Oscar Lewis. *Current Anthropology* 8, no. 5, Part 1 (Dec., 1967): 480–500, p. 499.

19   Small, M.L., Harding, D.J. & Lamont, M. 2010: 10.

20   See also Oestigaard, T. 2014. *Religion at Work in Globalised Traditions. Rainmaking, Witchcraft and Christianity in Tanzania.* Cambridge Scholars Publishing. Newcastle. This book discusses the consequences of lost traditions, which also includes the revival of witchcraft.

21   See UNESCO. 1972. Convention Concerning the Protection of the World Cultural and Natural Heritage. Paris: UNES. (accessed

7 March 2018). http://whc.unesco.org/en/ conventiontext/. The scholarly works on heritage studies is vast, but see for instance: Sontum, K. H. & Fredriksen, P. D. 2018. When The Past is slipping. Value tensions and responses by heritage management to demographic changes: a case study from Oslo, Norway. *International Journal of Heritage Studies*, Vol. 24, No. 4: 406-420; Holtorf, C. and Högberg, A. 2015. Contemporary Heritage and the Future. In Waterton, E. and Watson, S. (eds.). *The Palgrave Handbook of Contemporary Heritage Research:* 509–523. Palgrave Macmillan. Basingstoke; Högberg, A., Holtorf, C., May, S. & Wollentz, G. 2017. No future in archaeological heritage management?, *World Archaeology*, 49:5, 639–647, DOI: 10.1080/00438243.2017.1406398

22 Brumfiel, E. M. 2003. It's A Material World: History, Artefacts, and Anthropology. *Annual Review of Anthropology*, Vol. 32(2003): 205–223, p. 207.

23 Barth, F. 1987 [1993]. *Cosmologies in the Making. A Generative Approach to Cultural Variation in Inner New Guinea.* Cambridge University Press. Cambridge, p. 84.

24 Barth 1987:72.

25 Insoll, T. 2005. Archaeology of Cult and Religion. In Renfrew, C. and Bahn, P. (eds.). *Archaeology: The Key Concepts:* 45–49. Routledge. London, p. 45.

26 Insoll, T. 2004. Are Archaeologists Afraid of Gods? Some Thoughts on Archaeology and Religion. In Insoll, T. (ed.). *Belief in the Past. The Proceedings of the Manchester Conference on Archaeology and Religion:* 1–6. BAR International Series 1212. Oxford, p. 3.

27 http://oxforddictionaries.com/definition/tradition (Accessed 5 June 2018)

28 Krokfors, C. 1995. Poverty, Environmental Stress and Culture as factors in African Migrations. In Baker, J. & Aida, T. A. (eds.). *The Migration Experience in Africa:* 54–64. The Nordic Africa Institute. Uppsala, p. 58.

29 Oyebade, A. 2000. The Study of Africa in Historical Perspective. In Falola, T. (ed.). Africa. Vol. 1. *African History Before 1885:* 7–22. Carolina Academic Press. Durham, North Carolina, p. 9.

30 Goody, J. 1986. *The Logic of Writing and the Organisation of Society.* Cambridge University Press. Cambridge.

31 Turner, B. 1991. *Religion and Social Theory.* Sage. London.

32 Heien, K. H. 2007. *Local Livelihoods and the Bujagali Hydro-Power Dam, Uganda.* MA-thesis. Faculty of Economics and Social Sciences. Agder University College. Kristiansand.

33 Byerley, A. 2005. *Becoming Jinja. The Production of Space and Making of Place in and African Industrial Town.* Department of Human Geography. Stockholm University. Stockholm, p. 1.

34 Vaidya, P. B. & Amtzis, W. 1996/1997. *Water is water.* Journal of South Asian Literature, Vol. 31/32, No. 1/2: 208.

35 Nussenzveig, H. M. 1977. The Theory of the Rainbow. *Scientific American*, 236: 116–127, p. 116.

36 Rodis-Lewis, G. 1998. *Descartes. His Life and Thoughts.* Cornell University Press. Ithaca and London, p. 98.

37 Finlay, R. 2007. Weaving the Rainbow: Visions of Color in World History. *Journal of World History*, Vol. 18, No. 4: 383–431, p. 383.

38 Wittgenstein, L. 1972. *Philosophical Investigations*, edited by Anscombe, G. E. M & von Wright, G. H. Blackwell. Oxford, p. 22.

39 Riley, C. A 1995. *Color Codes. Modern Theories of Color in Philosophy, Painting and Architecture, Literature, Music, and Psychology.* University Press of New England. Hanover and London, p. 26.

40 Finlay 2007: 384, 387.

41 Bishop, R. L. & Newton, I. 1981. Rainbow over Woolsthorpe. *Notes and Records of the Royal Society of London*, Vol. 36, No. 1: 1–11, p. 3.

42 Epstein, J. L. & Greenberg, M. L. 1984. Decomposing Newton's Rainbow. *Journal of the History of Ideas*, Vol. 45, No. 1: 115–140, p. 118.

43   Finlay 2007: 431.

44   Newton, I. 1704. *Opticks: or, a treatise of the reflexions, refractions, inflexions and colours of light.* Also two treatises of the species and magnitude of curvilinear figures. Sam Smith & Benj. Walford. London, p. 126, 131.

45   Epstein & Greenberg 1984: 115–116.

46   Epstein & Greenberg 1984: 122.

47   op. cit. Hughes-Hallett, P. 2002. The Mystery of the Rainbow. *New England Review*, Vol. 23, No. 4: 131–145, p. 134.

48   Goethe, J. W. 1840. *Goethe's Theory of Colours.* Translated from the German: with notes by Charles Lock Eastlake. John Murray. London, p. 298, 162, 391.

49   Gigante, D. 2002. The Monster in the Rainbow: Keats and the Science of Life. *PMLA*, Vol. 17, No. 3: 433–448, p. 433.

50   Stillinger, J. (ed.). 1978. *The Poems of John Keats.* Part II. Cambridge. Massachusetts, p. 229–237.

51   Dawkins, R. 1998. *Unweaving the Rainbow.* Science, Delusion and the Appetite for Wonder. Houghton Mifflin. Boston, Massachusetts.

52   Finlay 2007: 398.

53   Finlay 2007: 400.

54   Lindberg, D. C. 1966. Roger Bacon's Theory of the Rainbow: Progress or Regress? *Isis*, Vol. 57, No. 2: 235–248, p. 242.

55   Meterol III.4. 375b, op.cit. Boyer, C. B. 1958a. The Tertiary Rainbow: An Historical Account. *Isis*, Vol. 49, No. 2: 141–154.

56   Boyer, C. B. 1958b. The Theory of the Rainbow: Medieval Triumph and Failure. *Isis*, Vol. 49, No. 4: 378–390, p. 378.

57   Boyer 1958b: 382.

58   Johnson, P. 2007. Proof of the Heavenly Iris: The Fountain of Three Rainbows at Wilton House, Wiltshire. *Garden History*, Vol. 35, No. 1: 51–67, p. 51, 61.

59   Johnson 2007: 52.

60   Schweizer, P. D. 1982. John Constable, Rainbow Science, and English Color Theory. *The Art Bulletin*, Vol. 64, No. 3: 424–445, p. 435.

61   Werrett, S. 2001. Wonders Never Cease: Descartes's "Météores" and the Rainbow Fountain. *The British Journal for the History of Science*, Vol. 34, No. 2: 129–147, p. 131.

62   Werrett 2001: 133.

63   Werrett 2001: 134.

64   op. cit. Werrett 2001: 141.

65   op. cit. Werrett 2001: 142.

66   Werrett 2001: 144.

67   Boyer, C. B. 1952. Descartes and the Radius of the Rainbow. *Isis*, Vol. 43, No. 2: 95–98.

68   Johnson 2007: 62.

69   Fisher, P. 1998. *Wonder, The Rainbow, and the Aesthetics of Rare Experiences.* Harvard University Press. Cambridge, p. 16.

70   Sarton, G. 1952. *Ancient Science Through the Golden Age of Greece.* Dover Publications, Inc. New York, p. 194.

71   Fisher 1998: 17.

72   Fisher 1998: 40.

73   Fisher 1998: 34, 37.

74   Lee & Fraser 2001: 111.

75   Pope, C. 1961. *The Giant Snakes. The Natural History of the Boa Constrictor, the Anaconda, and the largest Pythons, including comparative facts about other snakes and basic information about reptiles in general.* Routledge and Kegan Paul. London, p. 89.

76   Pope 1961: 199.

77   Op. cit. Stothers, R. B. 2004. Ancient Scientific Basis of the "Great Serpent" from Historical Evidence. *Isis*, Vol. 95, No. 2 (June 2004): 220–238, p. 224.

78   Murphy, J. C. & Henderson, R. W. 1997. *Tales of Giant Snakes. A Natural History of Anacondas and Pythons.* Krieger Publishing Company. Malabar, Florida, p. 23–24.

79   Pope 1961:152–153.

80   Murphy & Henderson 1997.

81   Murphy & Henderson 1997: 44–51.

82   Pope 1961: 14–17.

83   Pope 1961: 154, 157.

84   Murphy & Henderson 1997: 47, 56.

85   Lissmann, H. W. 1950. Rectilinear Locomotion in a Snake (Boa Occidentalis). *Journal of Experimental Biology* 1950 26: 368–379.

86   Murphy & Henderson 1997: 71.

87   Murphy & Henderson 1997: 87, 98–99.

88   Murphy & Henderson 1997: 131.

89   Pope 1961: 209.

90   Murphy & Henderson 1997: 79.

91   Lurker, M. 2005. Snakes. *In Encyclopedia of Religion*, Vol. 12: 8456–8460. Second Edition. Thomson Gale. Detroit, p. 8456.

92   e.g. Auliya, M. et al. 2002. Review of the reticulated python (Python reticulatus Schneider, 1801) with the description of new subspecies from Indonesia. *Naturwissenschaften.* 2002 May; 89(5): 201–13; Barker, D. G. et al. 2012. The Corrected Lengths of Two Well-known Giant Pythons and the Establishment of a New Maximum Length Record for Burmese Pythons, Python bivittatus. *Bull. Chicago Herp. Soc.* 47(1):1–6.

93   Mundkur, B. 1978. The Roots of Ophidian Symbolism. *Ethos*, Vol. 6, No. 3: 125–158, p. 136.

94   Hambly, W. D. 1929. The Serpent in African Belief and Custom. *American Anthropologist, New Series*, Vol. 31, No. 4: 655–666, p. 656.

95   Weissenborn, J. 1906a. Animal-Worship in Africa. *Journal of the Royal African Society*, Vol. 5, No. 18: 167–181, p. 180.

96   Weissenborn 1906a: 180.

97   Hambly 1929:6 64.

98   Shine, R. et al. 1998. The Influence of Sex and Body Size on Food Habits of a Giant Tropical Snake, Python reticulatus. *Functional Ecology*, Vol. 12, No. 2: 248–258, p. 249.

99   Starin, E. & Burghardt, G. M. 1982. African rock pythons Python sebae in the Gambia observations on natural history and interactions with Primates. *Snake.* August; 241: 50–62.

100 Kenny, M. G. 1977. The Powers of Lake Victoria. *Anthropos*, Bd. 72, H. 5/6: 717–733, p. 727.

101 Loewenstein, J. 1961. Rainbow and Serpent. *Anthropos*, Bd. 56, H. 1./2. (1961): 31–40, p. 32.

102 Loewenstein 1961: 33.

103 Saetersdal, T. 2010. Rain, Snakes and Sex – Making Rain: Rock Art and Rain-making in Africa and America. In Tvedt, T. & Oestigaard, T. (eds.). *A History of Water. Series 2, Vol. 1. Ideas of Water from Antiquity to Modern Times*: 378–404. I.B. Tauris. London, p. 400.

104 Loewenstein 1961: 35, 36.

105 Schebesta, P. 1950. *Die Bambuti-Pygmäen vom Ituri.* Roy. Colonial Belge 2. Brussels, p. 156.

106 Staniland Wake, C. 1873. The Origin of Serpent-Worship. *The Journal of the Anthropological Institute of Great Britain and Ireland*, Vol. 2(1873): 373–390.

107 Wang, E. Y. 2005. *Mirror, Moon, and Memory in Eighth-Century China: From Dragon Pond to Lunar Palace.* Cleveland Studies in the History of Art, Vol. 9 (Clarity and Luster: *New Light on Bronze Mirrors in tang and Post-Tang Dynasty China*, 600–1300: Papers from a Symposium on the Carter Collection of Chinese Bronze Mirrors at the Cleveland Museum of Art): 42–67, p. 44.

108 Hopkins, L. C. 1931. Where the rainbow Ends (An Introduction to the Dragon Terrestrial and the Dragon Celestial). *The Journal of the Royal Asiatic Society of Great Britain and Ireland*, No. 3: 603–612, p. 604.

109 Hopkins 1931: 605.

110 Lee & Fraser 2001: 27.

111 Jung, C. G. 1959. Forward. In Jacobi, J. *Complex/Archetype/Symbol. In the psychology of C. G. Jung:* ix–xi. Routledge and Kegan Paul. London, p. x, see also Jung, C. G. 1968a. *The Psychology of the Child Archetype. In The Archetypes and the Collective Unconscious.* The Collected Works Volume 9, Part 1: 151–181. Routledge and Kegan Paul. London; Jung, C. G. 1968b. *Concerning the Archetypes, with Special Reference to the Anima Concept. In The Archetypes and the Collective Unconscious.* The Collected Works Volume 9, Part 1: 54–74. Routledge and Kegan Paul; London; Jung, C. G. 1968c. *Psychological Aspects of the Mother Archetype. In The Archetypes and the Collective Unconscious.* The Collected Works Volume

9, Part 1: 75–110. Routledge and Kegan Paul. London.

112 Jung 1959:x–xi.

113 Jacobi, J. 1959. *Complex/Archetype/Symbol in the psychology of C. G. Jung.* Routledge and Kegan Paul. London, p. 51.

114 Blust, R. 2000. The Origins of Dragons. *Anthropos*, Bd. 95, H. 2 (2000): 519–536.

115 Ingersoll, E. 1928. *Dragons and Dragon Lore.* Payson and Clarke. New York, p. 13.

116 Blust 2000: 525.

117 Blust 2000: 525.

118 Blust 2000: 526.

119 Blust 2000: 529, 534.

120 Eliade, M. 1973. *Australian Religions: An Introduction.* Cornell University Press. Ithaca, New York, p. 115–116.

121 Lee & Fraser 2001: 22.

122 Radcliffe-Brown, A. R. 1926. The Rainbow-Serpent Myth of Australia. *The Journal of the Royal Anthropological Institute of Great Britain and Ireland,* Vol. 56: 19–25, p. 19.

123 Radcliffe-Brown 1926: 24–25.

124 Brumbaugh, R. 1987. The Rainbow Serpent on Upper Sepik. *Anthropos*, Bd. 82, H. 1/3: 25–33, p. 26.

125 Worms, E. A. 1955. Contemporary and Prehistoric Rock Paintings in Central and Northern Kimberley. *Anthropos*, Bd. 50, H. 4/6: 546–566, p. 548.

126 Taçon, P. S. C. 1991. The power of stone: symbolic aspects of stone use and tool development in western Arnhem Land, Australia. *Antiquity* 65 (1991): 192–207, p. 197.

127 Taçon 1991: 197.

128 Taçon 1991: 198.

129 Taçon 1991: 205.

130 Taçon, P. S. C., Wilson, M. & Chippindale, C. 1996. Birth of the rainbow Serpent in Arnhem Land rock art and oral history. *Archaeology in Oceania*, Vol. 31: 103–124.

131 Taçon, Wilson & Chippindale 1996: 103.

132 Oestigaard, T. in press. Waterfalls and moving waters: the unnatural natural and flows of cosmic forces. In Day, J. and Skeates, R. (eds.). *Routledge Handbook of Sensory Archaeology.* Routledge. London.

133 Taylor, L. 1990. The Rainbow Serpent as visual metaphor in western Arnhem Land. *Oceania* 60: 329–44.

134 Anderson, S. 2001. Rejecting the rainbow Serpent: An Aboriginal Artist's Choice of the Christian God as Creator. *The Australian Journal of Anthropology*, 12(3): 291–301, p. 296.

135 Taçon, P.S.C. 2008. Rainbow colour and power among the Waanyis of Northwest Queensland. *Cambridge Archaeological Journal* 18(2): 163–176.

136 Mountford, C. P. 1956. *Art, Myth and Symbolism: Records of the American – Australian Expedition to Arnhem Land,* Vol. 1. Melbourne University Press. Melbourne, p. 214.

137 Taylor, L. 2012. Connections of Spirit: Kuninjku Attachments to Country. In Weir, J. K. (ed.). *Country, Native Title and Ecology:* 21–45. ANU Press. Canberra.

138 Taylor, L. 2008. 'They May Say Tourist, May Say Truly Painting': Aesthetic Evolution and Meaning of Bark Paintings in Western Arnhem Land, Northern Australia. *The Journal of the Royal Anthropological Institute*, Vol. 14, No. 4: 865–885, p. 870, 877.

139 Lurker 2005: 8458–8459.

140 Wrigley, C. 1988. The River-God and the Historians. Myth in the Shire Valley and Elsewhere. *The Journal of African History*, Vol. 29, No. 3: 267–383, p. 372.

141 Hoff, A. 1997. The water Snake of the Khoekhoen and /Xam. *The South African Archaeological Bulletin*, Vol. 52, No. 165: 21–37.

142 Sarapik, V. 1998. Rainbow, Colours and Science Mythology. *Folklore* 6: 7–19, p. 9.

143 Holmberg, U. 1916. *The Mythology of All Races,* Vol. 4. Finno-Ugric, Siberian. Archaeological Institute of America. Boston, p. 444.

144 Meserve, H. C. 1987. Editorial: Searching for the Rainbow's End. *Journal of Religion and Health*, Vol. 26, No. 1: 3–8, p. 3.

138 | Terje Oestigaard

145 Witzel, M. 2015. *Water in Mythology.* Dædalus, the Journal of the American Academy of Arts & Sciences: 18–26, p. 22.

146 Barnes, R. H. 1973. The Rainbow in the Representations of Inhabitants of the Flores Area of Indonesia. *Anthropos*, Bd. 68, H. 3/4: 611–613.

147 Lee & Fraser 2001: viii.

148 Lee & Fraser 2001: 4–13.

149 Wessing, R. 2006. Symbolic Animals in the Land between Waters: Markers of Place and Transition. *Asian Folklore Studies*, Vol. 65, No. 2: 205-239.

150 Thankappan Nair, P. 1974. The Peacock Cult in Asia. *Asian Folklore Studies*, Vol. 33, No. 2: 93–170, p. 102.

151 Sarapik 1998: 8.

152 Lee & Fraser 2001: 29.

153 Lee & Fraser 2001: 25, 26.

154 Murphy & Henderson 1997: 169.

155 Turner, L. A. 1993. The Rainbow as the Sign of the Covenant in the Genesis IV 11–13. *Vetus Testamentum*, Vol. 43, Fasc. 1 (Jan., 1993): 119–124, p. 119–120.

156 Oestigaard, T. & Gedef, A. F. 2013. *The Source of the Blue Nile – Water Rituals and Traditions in the Lake Tana Region.* Cambridge Scholars Publishing. Newcastle, p. 66.

157 Turner 1993: 120–121.

158 Lorberbaum, Y. 2009. The Rainbow in the Cloud: An Anger-Management Device. *The Journal of Religion*, Vol. 89, No. 4: 498–540, p. 524.

159 Lorberbaum 2009: 534.

160 Dickow, H. & Møller, V. 2002. South Africa's "Rainbow People", National Pride and Optimism: A Trend Study. *Social Indicators Research*, Vol. 59, No. 2: 175–202.

161 Smith, E. W. 1952. African Symbolism. *The Journal of the Royal Anthropological Institute of Great Britain and Ireland,* Vol. 82, No. 1: 13–37, p.17.

162 Underhill, E. 1912. *Mysticism. A study in the nature and development of man's spiritual consciousness.* Dutton. New York, p. 95.

163 Smith 1952: 13–14.

164 Whitehead, A. N. 1927. *Religion in the Making.* Cambridge at the University Press. Cambridge, p. 117.

165 Jacobi, J. 1951. *The Psychology of C. G. Jung: An Introduction with Illustrations.* Routledge. London, p. 114.

166 Lévi-Strauss, C. 1969. *The Raw and the Cooked.* The University of Chicago Press. Chicago, p. 246

167 Todd, L. 1984. Review *The Drunken King, or, the Origin of the State by Luc de Heusch and Roy Willis. Folklore,* Vol. 95, No. 1: 129–130, p. 130.

168 Galaty, J. G. 1984. *Review The Drunken King or the Origin of the State by Luc De Heusch and Roy Willis. American Ethnologist,* Vol. 11, No. 3: 603–604.

169 Heusch, L. de. 1982. *The Drunken King or the Origin of the State. Translated and annotated by Roy Willis.* Indiana University Press. Bloomington.

170 Glazier, J. 1984. Review *The Drunken King, or the Origin of the State by Luc de Heusch and Roy Willis. The Journal of American Folklore,* Vol. 97, No. 383: 71–73, p. 72.

171 Heusch 1982: 8.

172 Heusch 1982: 35–36.

173 Heusch 1982: 37.

174 Heusch 1982: 39.

175 Heusch 1982: 42.

176 Heusch 1982: 55.

177 M'Kenzie, D. 1907. Children and Wells. *Folklore,* Vol. 18, No. 3: 253–282, p. 267.

178 See Drewal, J. H. 1988a. Mermaids, Mirrors, and Snake Charmers: Igbo Mami Wata Shrines. *African Arts,* Vol. 21, No. 2: 38–45+96; Drewal, J. H. 1988b. Performing the Other: Mami Wata Worship in Africa. *TDR,* Vol. 32, No. 2: 160–185.

179 Eliade, M. 1993. *Patterns in Comparative Religion*. Sheed and Ward Ltd. London, p. 193.

180 Hobley, C. W. 1929. *Kenya: From Chartered Company to Crown Colony. Thirty years of exploration and administration in British East Africa*. H.F. & G. Witherby. London, p. 113–114.

181 Hambly 1929: 658.

182 Hambly 1929: 657.

183 Weissenborn, J. 1906b. Animal-Worship in Africa (Concluded from p. 181). *Journal of the Royal African Society*, Vol. 5, No. 18: 269–289, p. 275.

184 Roscoe, J. 1911. *The Baganda. An Account of Their Native Customs and Beliefs*. Macmillan and Co. London, p. 318.

185 Roscoe 1911: 320–321.

186 Roscoe, J. 1909. Python Worship in Uganda. *Man*, Vol. 9 (1909): 88–90.

187 Roscoe 1911: 321.

188 Roscoe 1911: 322.

189 Kodesh, N. 2007. *History from the Healer's Shrine: Genre, Historical Imagination, and Early Ganda History*. Comparative Studies in Society and History, Vol. 49, No. 3: 527–552, p. 542, 544.

190 Hambly 1929: 660.

191 Lurker 2005: 8456.

192 Oestigaard 2015.

193 Oestigaard 2018.

194 See Gonza, R. K. et al. 2001. *Reconciliation among the Busoga*. Cultural Research Centre. Jinja; Gonza, R. K. et al. 2002. *Traditional Religion and Clans Among the Busoga*. Vol. 1. Cultural Research Centre. Jinja; Gonza, R. K. et al. 2003. *Witchcraft, Divination and Healing among the Basoga*. Cultural Research Centre. Jinja; Gonza, R. K. et al. 2010. *The Concept of Good Luck and Bad Luck among the Basoga*. Marianum Publishing Company. Kisubi.

195 Gonza et al. 2002: 135–137.

196 Gonza et al. 2010: p. 4.

197 Gonza et al. 2002: 149.

198 Gonza et al. 2002: 174.

199 Gonza 2010: 6.

200 Gonza et al. 2010: 111.

201 Kenny 1977: 719.

202 http://www.monitor.co.ug/Business/ World-Bank-decide-Bujagali-Isimba-dam-row/688322-3805150-15tgyje/index.html (accessed 10 April 2017) og mer informasjon om avtalen her, sjekk original

203 The literature on sacrifice is vast, see for instance Carrasco, D. 1999. City of Sacrifice. *The Aztec Empire and the Role of Violence in Civilization*. Beacon Press. Boston; Faherty, R. L. 1974. *Sacrifice*. The New Encyclopaedia Britannica. 15th ed. Macropaedia. Vol. 16: 128–135; Hubert, H. & Mauss, M. 1964. *Sacrifice: Its Nature and Function*. The University of Chicago Press. Chicago; Modéus, M. 2005. Sacrifice and Symbol. *Biblical Šelāmîm in a Ritual Perspective*. Coniectanea Biblica Old Testament Series 52. Almquist and Wiksell International. Stockholm; Read, K. A. 1998. *Time and sacrifice in the Aztec Cosmos*. Indiana University Press. Bloomington; Valeri, V. 1985. *Kingship and Sacrifice. Ritual and Society in Ancient Hawaii*. The University Press of Chicago. Chicago.

204 Sanders, T. 2008. *Beyond Bodies. Rainmaking and Sense Making in Tanzania*. Toronto University Press. Toronto, p.: xiii.

205 Tvedt, T. & Oestigaard, T. 2016. *Approaches to African Food Production in a Water Society Systems Perspective*. In Tvedt, T. & Oestigaard, T. (eds.). *A History of Water*, Series 3, Volume 3. *Water and Food: From Hunter-Gatherers to Global Production in Africa*: 1–25. I.B. Tauris. London, p. 9–10.

206 https://waterpolls.org/world-economic-forum-survey-water/ (Accessed 7 June 2018)

207 See Oestigaard 2018, chapter 4.

208 Saetersdal, T. 2009. *Manica Rock-Art in Contemporary Society*. In Oestigaard, T. (ed.). 2009. *Water, Culture and Identity. Comparing Past and Present Traditions in the Nile Basin Region*: 55–82. BRIC Press. Bergen.

209 It is here impossible to refer to everyone who has been studying rainmaking in Africa since it has been intrinsic part of the past and present, and parts of the ethnographic studies with particular relevance to the Nile basin will be used in the following discussion. For studies of the past, see for instance Aukema, J. 1989. Rain-making: a thousand year old ritual. *South African Archaeological Bulletin* 44: 70–72; Dowson, T. A. 1993. Rain in Bushman belief, politics and history; the rock-art of rain-making in the southeastern mountains, southern Africa. In Chippendale, C. and Taçon, P.S.C. (eds.) *The archaeology of Rock-Art:* 73–89. University of Cambridge Press. Cambridge; Lan, D. 1985. *Guns and rain: guerillas and spirit mediums in Zimbabwe.* James Currey ltd. London; Lewis-Williams, D. 1977. *Led by the nose: observations on the supposed use of southern San rock art in rain-making rituals.* African studies 36: 155–159; Nhamo, A. Saetersdal, T. & Walderhaug, E. 2007. Ancestral Landscapes. Reporting on Rock Art in the border regions between Zimbabwe and Mozambique. In: *Zimbabwea, Special Issue,* Number 9. *National Museums and Monuments of Zimbabwe.* Harare; Schapera, I. 1971. *Rain-making rites of Tswana tribes.* African Social Research Documents – Volume 3, African studies centre, Cambridge; Schmidt, I. 1979. The Rain Bull of the South African Bushmen. *African Studies* Vol. 38: 201–224, and Schoeman, M. H. 2006. Imagining rain-places: Rain-control and changing ritual landscapes in the Shashe-Limpopo Confluence Area, South Africa. *The South African Archaeological Bulletin,* Vol 61. Number 184: 152–165. See also references to Saetersdal later.

210 Tvedt, T. 2016. *Water and Society – Changing Perceptions of Societal and Historical Development.* I.B. Tauris. London, p. 65.

211 See Oestigaard, T. 2003. *An Archaeology of Hell: Fire, Water and Sin in Christianity.* Bricoleur Press. Lindome; Oestigaard, T. 2005. *Water and World Religions. An Introduction.* SFU & SMR. Bergen; Oestigaard, T. 2008. The Sisters Kali and Ganga: Waters of Life and Death. In Håland, E. (ed.). *Women, Pain and Death: Rituals and Everyday Life on the Margins of Europe and Beyond:* 203–221. Cambridge Scholars Publishing. Newcastle upon Tyne; Oestigaard, T. (ed.). 2009. *Water, Culture and Identity. Comparing Past and Present Traditions in the Nile Basin Region.* BRIC Press. Bergen; Oestigaard, T. 2010. Purification, Purgation and Penalty: Christian Concepts of Water and Fire in Heaven and Hell. In Tvedt, T. & Oestigaard, T. (eds.). A *History of Water.* Series 2, Vol. 1. *The Ideas of Water from Antiquity to Modern Times:* 298–322. I.B. Tauris. London, and Oestigaard, T. 2011. Water. In Insoll, T. (ed.). *The Oxford Handbook of the Archaeology of Ritual and Religion:* 38–50. Oxford University Press. Oxford.

212 Human Development Report 2006. *Beyond scarcity: Power, poverty and the global water crisis.* UNDP. New York, p. 174.

213 Skarstein, R. 2016. Primitive Accumulation: Concept, Similarities and Varieties. In Havnevik, K., Oestigaard, T., Virtanen, T. & Tobisson, E. (eds.). *Framing African Development. Challenging Concepts:* 135–168. Brill. Leiden, p. 150.

214 Oestigaard 2018, chapter 4.

215 Lefebvre, H. 1997. The Production of Space. In Leach, N. (ed.). *Rethinking Architecture. A reader in cultural theory:* 139–147. Routledge. London, p. 139.

216 Lefebvre 1997: 140.

217 Lucas, G. 1995. Interpretation in contemporary archaeology: some philosophical issues. In Hodder, I. et al. (eds.). *Interpreting archaeology: Finding meaning in the past:* 37–44. Routledge. London.

218 See for instance Miller, D. 1985. *Artefacts as Categories: A Study of Ceramic Variability in Central India.* Cambridge University Press. Cambridge; Miller, D. 1987. *Material Culture and Mass Consumption.* Basil Blackwell. Oxford; Miller, D. 1994. Artefacts and the meaning of things. In Ingold, T. (ed.) Companion encyclopedia of anthropology, pp. 396–419. Routledge. London; Miller, D. 1998. Introduction: Why some things matter. In Miller, D. (ed.). *Material cultures – Why some things matter,* pp. 3–21. University College

London Press. London, and Miller, D. & Tilley, C. 1996. Editorial. *Journal of Material Culture* Vol. 1, No. 1: 5–14

[219] Miller 1994: 398, p. 400.

[220] Leclerc, I. 2014. *The Nature of Physical Existence.* Routledge. London, p. 122.

[221] Tshimanga, R. M. 2009. Traditional Values and Uses of Water along the upper Congo River. In Oestigaard, T. (ed.). *Water, Culture and Identity. Comparing Past and Present Traditions in the Nile Basin Region:* 21–51. BRIC Press. Bergen; Tshimanga, R. M. 2010. *Traditional Systems of Water and water Resources Management along the Upper Congo River.* Fountain Publishers. Kampala, and Tshimanga, R. M. 2016. Water and food systems in the Congo rainforest. In Tvedt, T. & Oestigaard, T. (eds.). *A History of Water,* Series 3, Vol. 3. *Water and Food: From hunter-gatherers to global production in Africa:* 355–368. I.B. Tauris. London.

[222] Struhsaker, T. T. 1997. *Ecology of an African rain forest. Logging in Kibale and the Conflict between Conservation and Exploitation.* University of Florida Press. Gainesville, p. 1.

[223] Turnbull, C. 1961. *The Forest People.* Simon and Schuster. New York.

[224] Turnbull, C. M. 1972[1987]. *The Mountain People.* Simon & Schuster. New York, p. 280, 284.

[225] Turnbull 1987[1972]: 135.

[226] Turnbull 1987[1972]: 202.

[227] Turnbull 1987[1972]: 269–270.

[228] Heine, B. 1985. The Mountain People: Some Notes on the Ik of North-eastern Uganda. *Africa: Journal of the International African Institute,* Vol. 55, No. 1: 3–16.

[229] Barth, F. 1974. On Responsibility and Humanity: Calling a Colleague to Account. Current Anthropology, Vol. 15, No. 1: 99–103, p. 100, 102.

[230] Knight, J. 1994. 'The Mountain People' as Tribal Mirror. *Anthropology Today,* Vol. 10, No. 6: 1–3.

[231] Oestigaard, T. 2016. Developing the 'Other' – Challenging Concepts. In Havnevik, K., Oestigaard, T., Tobisson, E. & Virtanen, T. 2016 (eds.). *Framing African Development. Challenging Concepts:* 16–34. Brill. Leiden.

[232] Tvedt, T. 2004. T*he River Nile in the Age of the British. Political Ecology and the Quest for Economic Power.* I.B. Tauris. London, p. 6.

[233] Gorman, R. 1982. *Neo-Marxism. The Meanings of Modern Radicalism.* Greenwood Press. London, p. 20. For a theoretical discussion of methodological collectivism and idealism and different positions, see for instance Elster, J. 1987. *Making Sense of Marx.* Cambridge University Press. Cambridge; Elster, J. 1989. *The Cement of Society. A Study of Social Order.* Cambridge. University Press. Cambridge; Gilje, N. & Grimen, H. 2001. *Samfunnsvitenskapenes forutsetninger. Innføring i samfunnsvitenskapenes vitenskapsfilosofi.* Universitetsforlaget. Oslo; Marx, K. 1970. *A contribution to the critique of political economy.* International Publishers. New York, and Watkins, J. W. N. 1973. Ideal types and historical explanation. In Ryan, A. (ed.). *The Philosophy of Social Explanation.* Oxford University Press. Oxford.

[234] Latour, B. 1993. *We Have Never Been Modern.* Prentice Hall. London; Latour, B. 1997. The Trouble with Actor-Network Theory. *Philosophia.* Vol. 25, No. 3–4: 47–64; Latour, B. 1999. *Pandora's Hope.* Essays on the Reality of Science Studies. Harvard University Press. Cambridge, MA, and Latour, B. 2003. Revolution. In Pepper, D., et al. (eds), *Environmentalism. Critical Concepts.* Vol. V: 287–327. Routledge. London.

[235] Latour 1993: 85.

[236] Bourdieu, P. 1977. *Outline of a theory of practice.* Cambridge University Press. Cambridge; Bourdieu, P. 1984. *Distinction: a social critique of the judgement of taste.* Harvard University Press. Cambridge, Mass; Bourdieu, P. 1995. *The Logic of Practice.* Polity Press. Oxford; Giddens, A. 1989. Sociology. Polity Press. Cambridge; and Giddens, A. 1999. Risk and Responsibility. *The Modern Law Review.* Vol. 62, No. 1: 1–10.

[237] Giddens 1999: 3.

[238] Tvedt 2016: 220–221.

[239] See also Tvedt, T. 2010a. Why England and not China and India? Water systems and the history of the industrial revolution. *Journal of Global History* Vol. 5: 29–50; Tvedt, T. 2010b. Water: a source of wars or a pathway to peace? An empirical critique of two dominant schools of thought on water and international politics. In Tvedt, T., Chapman, G. & Hagen, R. (eds). *A History of Water,* Series 3, Vol. 3 *Water, Geopolitics and the New World Order:* 78–108. I.B.Tauris. London; Tvedt, T. 2010c. Water systems, environmental history and the deconstruction of nature, *Environment and History,* Vol. 16: 143–66; Tvedt, T. 2011. Hydrology and empire: The Nile, water imperialism and the partition of Africa. *The Journal of Imperial and Commonwealth History,* Vol. 39, No. 2: 173–94.

[240] Erlich, H. & Gershoni, I. 2000. Introduction. In Erlich, H. & Gershoni, I. (eds), *The Nile: Histories, Cultures, Myths:* 1–14. Lynne Rienner Publishers. Boulder, CO and London.

[241] Oyebade 2000: 7.

[242] Falola, T. 2002. Introduction. In Falola, T. (ed.). Africa Vol. 3. *Colonial Africa, 1885–1939:* xvii–xxiii. Carolina Academic Press. Durham, North Carolina, p. xviii.

[243] Hegel, G. W. F. 2007[1899]. *The Philosophy of History.* Cosimo. New York, p. 99.

[244] Hegel 2007[1899]: 98.

[245] Ba, D. 2007. *Africans still seething over Sarkozy speech.* http://uk.reuters.com/article/2007/09/05/uk-africa-sarkozy-idUKL0513034620070905 (accessed 1 October 2012)

[246] Fage, J. D. & Oliver, R. 1978. Preface. In Fage, J. D. & Oliver, R. (ed.). *The Cambridge History of Africa.* Volume 2. From c. 500 BC to AD 1050: xiv–xvi. Cambridge University Press. Cambridge.

[247] Fage, J. D. 1978. Introduction. In Fage, J. D. & Oliver, R. (ed.). *The Cambridge History of Africa.* Volume 2. From c. 500 BC to AD 1050: 1–10. Cambridge University Press. Cambridge, p. 6, my emphasis.

[248] Fage 1978: 10.

[249] Fuglestad, F. 1992. The Trevor-Roper Trap or the Imperialism of History. An Essay. *History in Africa,* Vol. 19: 309–326, p. 310.

[250] Trevor-Roper, H. 1965. *The Rise of Christian Europe.* Thames and Hudson. London, p. 9.

[251] Trevor-Roper 1965: 9.

[252] Trevor-Roper 1965:9-10.

[253] Trevor-Roper 1965:11.

[254] Trevor-Roper, H. 1969. The Past and the Present. History and Sociology. *The Past and Present Society,* No. 42: 3–17, p. 6.

[255] Fuglestad 1992: 312–313.

[256] Trigger, B. 1984. Archaeologies: Nationalist, Colonialist, Imperialist. *Man,* New Series, Vol. 19, No. 3: 355–370, p. 363.

[257] Trigger 1984:360.

[258] See for instance Nyamnjoh, F. 2016. *#RhodesMustFall: Nibbling at Resilient Colonialism in South Africa.* Langaa. Bamenda, Melber, H. 2018. Knowledge production and decolonisation – Not only African challenges. *Strategic Review for Southern Africa,* Vol. 40, No. 1: 4–15.

[259] Ndlovu-Gatsheni, S. J. 2018. The Dynamics of Epistemological Decolonisation in the 21st Century: Towards Epistemic Freedom. *Strategic Review for Southern Africa,* Vol. 40, No. 1: 16–45, p. 17.

[260] Chilisa, B. 2012. *Indigenous Research Methodologies.* Sage. Los Angeles/London/New Delhi, p. 14.

[261] Comaroff, J. & Comaroff, J. L. 2012. *Theory From the South Or, How Euro-America Is Evolving Toward Africa.* Paradigm Publishers. Boulder and London, p. 1.

[262] Wenke, R. 2009. *The Ancient Egyptian State: The Origins of Egyptian Culture* (c. 8000–2000 bc). Cambridge University Press. Cambridge, p. 80.

[263] Tvedt, T. 2012. *Nilen – historiens elv.* Aschehoug. Oslo, p. 101.

[264] Source: Ingela Dahlin, librarian at the Nordic Africa Institute. Databases were checked 6 March 2018.

265 Mkandawire, T. 2002. "African Intellectuals, Political Culture and Development". *Austrian Journal of Development Studies*, Vol. 18, No. 1: 31–47, p. 25.

266 Speke, J. H. 1863. *Journal of the Discovery of the Source of the White Nile*. Blackwood and Sons. Edinburgh and London; Speke, J. H. 1864. *What Led to the Discovery of the Source of the Nile*. Blackwood and Sons. Edinburgh and London.

267 Filippi, F. de. 1908. Ruwenzori. *An account of the expedition of H.R.H. Prince Luigi Amedeo of Savoy duke of the Abruzzi*. Archibald Constable and Company Limited. London, p. 44.

268 Berry, S. 1993. *No Condition is Permanent. The Social Dynamics of Agrarian Change in Sub-Saharan Africa*. The University of Wisconsin Press. Wisconsin, p. 8.

269 Ingold, T. 2000. *The Perception of the Environment*. Routledge. London, p. 216.

270 Jones, O. and Cloke, P. 2002. *Three Cultures*. Berg. Oxford, p. 77.

271 Oestigaard 2018, chapter 3.

272 http://www.crcjinja.org/aboutus.html (accessed 30 May 2018)

273 e.g. Gonza et. al. 2001, 2002, 2003, 2010. See also Oestigaard 2015, 2018.

274 Turner 1991.

Index

Before the rains can be released from the sky as a divine gift, making a beautiful rainbow in the sky, Mesoké himself has to bring the waters to the sky. And that happens through the rainbow.
Photo: Terje Oestigaard

9 789171 068477